Human Interest Stories of the Gettysburg Campaign

Volume 2

Scott L. Mingus, Sr.

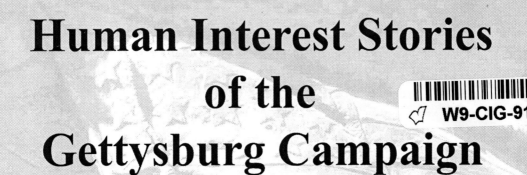

Colecraft Industries
Since 1981

Published by Colecraft Industries
970 Mt. Carmel Road
Orrtanna, PA 17353

The author wishes to thank the staff of the U.S. Army Military History Institute, who provided leads on materials in their library and files, as did the library of the Gettysburg National Military Park, the University of North Carolina, and various historical societies. Most of all, thanks to my beloved wife Debi for her unwavering support, understanding, and encouragement.

ISBN 0-9777125-40

For more information please contact us via e-mail at: **colecraftbooks@aol.com**
or
Visit us at: **colecraftbooks.com**

First Edition

PRINTED AND BOUND IN THE UNITED STATES OF AMERICA

Cover Design by Philip M. Cole

Contents

Introduction   4

Chapter One: The Confederates Invade Pennsylvania   5

Chapter Two: The Battle of Gettysburg - Wednesday,   34
        July 1, 1863

Chapter Three: The Battle of Gettysburg - Thursday,   49
        July 2, 1863

Chapter Four: The Battle of Gettysburg - Friday,   64
        July 3, 1863

Chapter Five: The Aftermath   79

Introduction

Over the past century and a half, perhaps a thousand books have related to or described the Battle of Gettysburg. Most seek to inform the reader of the movements of the respective armies, the ebb and flow of the three-day conflict, and its aftermath. Some focus on the leaders, some on the regiments and brigades, some on the civilian populace and area landmarks, and others on the strategy and tactics. Only a handful, however, have portrayed the battle from the perspective of the individual soldiers and residents. More than 170,000 men fought at Gettysburg, a community of fewer than 3,000 people in 1863. It is their stories I have pored through and distilled into this collection of incidents, anecdotes, and affairs of ordinary people at Gettysburg. Inside these pages, you will find accounts of courage, of fear and failure, of irony and humor. Most have not appeared in print for nearly a century. All are deemed to be true, although it must be admitted the memories of veterans dimmed with time, and stories of their exploits correspondingly grew in stature and hyperbole. Still, these tales serve to illustrate the plight of the common foot-soldier at Gettysburg, many of whom survived the battle to write about it in later years.

The Civil War was a time of chaos, conflict, and carnage. Untold millions of Americans can trace their ancestry to men who wore the Blue and the Gray. While we can never know these soldiers from long ago, we can get a perception of their mindsets and a glimpse of their daily lives through the nearly two hundred incidents in this collection, a companion and addendum to the popular *Human Interest Stories of the Gettysburg Campaign*. It is my humble way of preserving some of their stories for another generation, helping us understand in some small way what it was like for the soldiers and civilians at Gettysburg.

This book is dedicated in honor of my beloved bride of thirty years, Debi, who is still my best friend and life companion. She has patiently endured my obsession with the Civil War and countless hours of tramping old battlefields. Her faith and encouragement have been a constant source of inspiration and comfort.

There is much left to tell about the ordinary men and women whose lives were forever impacted by the Battle of Gettysburg. Feel free to send me stories of your ancestors from letters, diaries, newspaper accounts, and other documentation of their heroism and military service during the Gettysburg Campaign. Send all e-mails to scottmingus@yahoo.com, and the editors and author will review your material for inclusion in possible upcoming volumes.

Scott Mingus
York, Pennsylvania

Chapter 1

The Confederates Invade Pennsylvania
June 1863

Confederate General Robert E. Lee invaded the North in September 1862, being stopped at the Battle of Antietam in northern Maryland. By the following spring, the Virginian believed another invasion was warranted and, following his startling victory at Chancellorsville in May, the timing was now right in his estimation. He had several goals in mind, including moving the seat of war from Virginia to the lush fields of Pennsylvania, where prosperous Northern farmers could feed the huge armies. He wanted to threaten or seize Harrisburg, the capital of the nation's second largest state, and sever communications and supply routes vital to the Union war effort. Should opportunity arise, perhaps he could threaten Baltimore or Washington and force the U.S. Army to divert troops from Vicksburg, Mississippi, to the East to counter his movements. Some in the Confederacy believed a decisive victory on Northern soil might encourage foreign intervention, or, at least, stir up enough anti-war, or "Copperhead," sentiment to force the Lincoln Administration to negotiate peace. Lee received the Confederate government's approval and then planned the final details of his expedition. He reorganized his army and prepared for the long trek northward.

With the death of Stonewall Jackson on May 10, Lee split his Second Corps into two smaller organizations, assigning these commands to Lieutenant Generals A.P. Hill and Richard S. Ewell. Some soldiers in the rank and file questioned these appointments. Ewell had been badly wounded the previous summer and was just now getting back to the army. His return was noted by Marylander Randolph McKim: "On Saturday, the 20th, General Ewell arrived in camp with his wife—a new acquisition—and with one leg less than when I saw him last. From a military point of view, the addition of the wife did not compensate for the loss of the leg. We were of the opinion that Ewell was not the same soldier he had been when he was a whole man—and a single one."

Randolph H. McKim, A Soldier's Recollections: Leaves from the Diary of a Young Confederate. (New York: Longmans, Green, and Co., 1910).

**

Starting on June 3, elements of Lee's Army of Northern Virginia broke camp near Fredericksburg in east-central Virginia and headed for Pennsylvania. Contradictory reports reached the Federal War Department, and Union cavalry scouts sent out to investigate, failed to verify the Rebels' intention. A few days later, once it had been confirmed that the

Confederates were indeed on the move, Major General Joseph Hooker's Union Army of the Potomac began pursuing Lee. Within a month, more than 170,000 men would converge at the small Pennsylvania crossroads borough of Gettysburg. For thousands of soldiers, it would be their final resting place.

The War of the Rebellion: A Compilation of the Official Records of the Union and Confederate Armies, 70 volumes in 4 series. Washington, D.C.: United States Government Printing Office, 1880-1901. Volume 39.

**

As the opposing armies advanced towards their unknown destinies at Gettysburg, they were accompanied by tens of thousands of animals, including light riding horses, sturdy draft horses, herds of beef cattle, and an array of stubborn mules. Soldiers' attitudes towards this massive aggregation of service animals were mixed, ranging from compassion and tender care to open neglect and abuse. As the 148th Pennsylvania marched from its camp in Falmouth, Virginia, northward towards Maryland, a mule became swamped in the morass as the regiment forded a stream. Unable to extricate itself, the heavy animal sank to the bottom and stuck fast, and the soldiers callously tramped on its back as they crossed the watercourse.

Private John English loaded a cartridge into his musket and placed the muzzle against one of the mule's ears. He squeezed the trigger, and the resulting blast ended the mule's struggles. Lieutenant Colonel Robert McFarlane heard the gunshot and galloped from the front of the column to investigate. Seeing the dead mule, he demanded to know who was guilty of this breach of military discipline. He received no reply, as everyone professed ignorance. A frustrated McFarlane gave up and sullenly rode back to the head of his regiment.

Joseph Wendel Muffly, The Story of Our Regiment: A History of the 148th Pennsylvania Vols. (Des Moines, Iowa: The Kenyon Printing & Mfg. Co., 1904).

**

Food was always on the minds of Civil War soldiers. They drew rations from the commissary wagons, but often foraged nearby farms to supplement the meager fare. The daily rations of Brigadier General George Steuart's Confederates in the early days of the campaign are illustrative—each man was issued a half-pound of salt-cured bacon and one and one-eighth pounds of flour. In addition, every one hundred men in a regiment split six pounds of sugar, fifteen pounds of peas, and three pounds of salt among them, along with two pounds of soap for personal hygiene.

Randolph H. McKim, A Soldier's Recollections: Leaves from the Diary of a Young Confederate. (New York: Longmans, Green, and Co., 1910).

One hot, oppressive day in early June, the 12th New Jersey marched toward Thoroughfare Gap in the Bull Run Mountains in central Virginia. In that region, shallow streams and brooks had dried up from a recent drought. The scorching heat caused the water in the men's tin canteens to reach an undrinkable temperature. With little other potable water available, soldiers dehydrated and became fatigued from the grueling march in unrelenting sunshine.

As the dusty column passed through the old Bull Run battlefield, murmurs of discontent rippled through the ranks. Many were now in a foul and complaining mood. Prodded along by their officers, the parched men dourly resumed the march. They passed by the decomposing body of a fallen soldier from the earlier battle. A lifeless arm eerily protruded, pointing skyward, from the mound of earth that marked his final resting place. One wag, with a penchant for absurd remarks, glimpsed the uplifted arm and shouted, "Say, boys, see that soldier putting out his hand for back pay!" The exclamation was infectious, and laughter rang out along the column as the men temporarily forgot their suffering.

Samuel Toombs, New Jersey Troops in the Gettysburg Campaign. (Orange, New Jersey: The Evening Mail Publishing House, 1888).

**

People were generally smaller in height and physical stature in the mid-19th Century than today's modern generation. People of unusual height or girth were often the object of amazement and amusement, much like a circus freak. One of the newer brigade commanders in the Army of the Potomac was Colonel John Irvin Gregg, a tall and lanky veteran of the Mexican-American War. Early in the Civil War, his men slipped around his headquarters to gawk at the towering Pennsylvanian. They were in awe of his commanding presence, particularly when they unexpectedly encountered him around a corner. At 6' 4", he soared over the average man. His troopers had many a good laugh at his expense, with gleeful exclamations such as "Golly! Wouldn't want to be so big, sure to get hit!", "My, couldn't he swing a saber! We've got the biggest colonel in the army." and "Whew! Isn't he a Long John!" The cavalrymen adopted "Long John" as the preferred nickname for their beloved leader, and now they followed him back into their native Pennsylvania. For some, it would be their last campaign.

Pennsylvania at Gettysburg: Ceremonies at the dedication of the monuments erected by the commonwealth of Pennsylvania... (Pennsylvania Battlefield Commission, 1913).

**

Lee's army steadily approached Northern soil as June wore on. Ewell's Corps streamed northward through Virginia's Shenandoah Valley and routed Federals near

Winchester and Martinsburg in mid-month, seizing thousands of prisoners, weapons, horses, and mountains of supplies. One Yankee wrote about his regiment's hasty departure from their camp near Berryville: "We dumped the bean soup onto the fire, set fire to the rest [of the supplies], and moved on." The same calamity was repeated at other Union camps. One gleeful North Carolina Rebel wrote, "The birds had flown," leaving behind plenty of edibles still cooking on hastily abandoned campfires. He added, "We ate all we could and filled our haversacks." Another fortunate Tar Heel "got plenty of coffee… and a good lot of letter paper."

L. Leon, Diary of a Tar Heel Confederate Soldier. (Charlotte, North Carolina: Stone Publishing Co., 1913).

**

Southern Pennsylvanians met at markets, mills, churches, stores, and in each others' parlors and porches to exchange the latest rumors about the oncoming Confederates. Wild tales spread that the Rebels were intent on murder and mayhem. Gettysburg school teacher Sallie Broadhead wrote in her diary on June 15 about the general sense of fear and anxiety in the borough, the seat of rural Adams County. "Our town had a great fright last night between 12 and 1 o'clock," noted the young mother of a four-year-old daughter. "I had retired, and was soundly asleep, when my child cried for a drink of water. When I got up to get it, I heard so great a noise in the street that I went to the window."

She was alarmed by the lurid glow from a large fire, seemingly close by. Worried citizens roamed the streets, calling, "The Rebels are coming, and burning as they go." It turned out that the mysterious conflagration was across the state line in Emmitsburg, Maryland, some ten miles south of Gettysburg. It had not been set by vengeful Confederates, but had started accidentally in a livery stable. The resulting inferno consumed over fifty buildings. The regrettable incident heightened concerns that the Rebels might harm private property.

Sarah M. Broadhead diary, files of the Library of the Gettysburg National Military Park.

**

Residents of the region bordering the Mason-Dixon Line, separating slave-state Maryland from free-state Pennsylvania, were no strangers to rumors of impending Rebel incursions. A number of small engagements and raids had occurred there during the first two years of the war. In September 1862, powerful infantry commands under Lieutenant General James Longstreet marched within ten miles of Pennsylvania before withdrawing to Sharpsburg and the subsequent Battle of Antietam. In October, J.E.B. Stuart's cavalry raided southern Pennsylvania, damaging railroads around Chambersburg and riding within a few miles of Gettysburg.

Thousands of young men in the area were now serving in the military, including large numbers of relatives. In McConnellsburg, well to the west of Gettysburg in Fulton County, every male of the Glenn family was in the Union army, including brothers James, John, Jacob, Andrew, and George, and their two brothers-in-law, David Montgomery and Henry Washabaugh. Numerous cousins and other kinfolk also had enlisted. And yet, as Confederates began entering Maryland and Pennsylvania, dozens of Southerners wrote home stating their surprise in seeing so many young Northern men of apparent health and vitality still living at home, having chosen not to enroll in the Federal army or having already been mustered out after their terms of enlistment had expired.

History of Cumberland and Adams Counties, Pennsylvania. (Chicago: Warner, Beers & Co., 1886).

**

Lee's army began crossing the Potomac River into Maryland while bands played *Maryland, My Maryland*. Confederate leaders expected to receive thousands of new recruits and substantial support from the populace. Both proved to be less than expected. On Thursday, June 17, George Steuart's brigade crossed the Potomac near Shepherdstown, West Virginia, at 2:30 p.m. General Steuart and his adjutant, Randolph McKim, rode side by side through the river into their native state. The general, nicknamed "Maryland" Steuart for his passionate love for his state, sprang from his horse, dropped to his hands and knees, and kissed the ground. He was home.

Randolph H. McKim, A Soldier's Recollections: Leaves from the Diary of a Young Confederate. (New York: Longmans, Green, and Co., 1910).

**

The first Confederates to enter Pennsylvania were Brigadier General Alfred Jenkins' mounted infantrymen, mostly partisans and rangers who were natives of the mountainous region that had recently become the state of West Virginia. After midnight on June 15, several advance scouts rode through the silent streets of Chambersburg, illuminated at that late hour only by gaslights in front of the bank. In the darkness, four or five soldiers became separated from the main body. One confused Rebel rode up to two townsmen on the sidewalk near the courthouse and, mistakenly thinking they were comrades, asked what direction the rest of the squad had gone. The civilians, in reality a pair of recently discharged Union soldiers, decided to try to capture the straggler. Neither man was armed, but T. M. Mahon brandished a plastering lath in one hand, simulating a sword. He grabbed one rein, while John Seiders seized the other one and quietly demanded the Rebel's surrender. Mahon grabbed the trooper's saber and one of his pistols, and then jumped onto the horse and headed out of town. Spotting more Rebel cavalry, he ducked into the market house (an open-sided wooden structure) and made good his escape after the Confederates rode by.

In the meantime, Seiders, wielding the other pistol, silently marched the embarrassed captive, George Hawkins, out of sight and turned him over to two bystanders to be escorted to the jail. Walking to the bank, Seiders heard a voice call out in a peculiar Southern tone, "Hawkins! Hawkins!! I say, Hawkins, whar in the devil are you?" After a brief pause, he heard, "Whar's the Mayaw [mayor] of this town? What's the Mayaw of this town? If the Mayaw does not come here in five minutes, we will burn the town." Seiders strolled over to the lone Confederate horseman, a lieutenant named Smith, presented the cocked pistol, and quietly demanded his surrender. A startled Smith complied and ruefully dismounted. Seiders disarmed him, taking his saber, pistols, and spurs.

Mounting Smith's horse, Seiders raced down East Market Street, leaving the stunned officer standing in the dimly lit avenue. Running into the main Confederate patrol, Seiders changed course. Ignoring their command to halt, he galloped out of town eastward to nearby Fayetteville. Arriving in the early morning, he dismounted and took inventory of his capture—a useful horse, a valuable leather saddle, four blankets rolled up and fastened behind the saddle, two fine pistols, a gleaming saber and belt, and a pair of saddlebags containing a Confederate officer's dress coat, two shirts, a testament, a pack of playing cards, a package of love letters, some smoking tobacco, and several other personal articles.

The next day, General Jenkins and his staff rode into Chambersburg and established headquarters at the Montgomery Hotel. Angered by reports of the theft of horses and accoutrements, the Virginian summoned the town council. He demanded the return of the missing animals and equipment, or required payment for their full value if they could not be produced. He threatened to burn the town if his orders were not met. Since the captured property was now well beyond the councilmen's reach, they agreed to settle the matter with a payment of $900. Doubtless, Jenkins expected this amount in United States currency, but, as he had earlier that morning flooded the town with Confederate scrip in payment for food and supplies, pronouncing it "better than greenbacks," the city fathers now took him at his word. Much to his chagrin, they paid most of the debt in his own money.

John Seiders performed well during the rest of the campaign as a volunteer spy, dressed in Lieutenant Smith's captured uniform coat. Afterwards, he sold the stolen horse for $175 and the saddle for $35. Out of this amount, he refunded the $75 the transaction had cost the council, leaving him a tidy $135 remainder. The gutsy and quick-thinking Seiders and Mahon were among the few fortunate Pennsylvanians to profit from the Confederate invasion.

Samuel P. Bates and Richard J. Fraise. History of Franklin County, Pennsylvania. (Chicago: Warner, Beers and Co., 1887).
Jacob Hoke, The Great Invasion. (Dayton, Ohio: W. J. Shuey, Publisher, 1887).

**

On June 20, Lieutenant Hermann Schuricht's company of the 14th Virginia Cavalry seized several horses, along with cattle, from Pennsylvania farmers. At noon, the Confederates rode into the farmyard of an old Pennsylvania German near Waynesboro, southeast of Chambersburg. Scared to death at the sight of the enemy horsemen, he shouted "O mein Gott, die rebels!" Schuricht assured the terrified farmer that he would not be harmed if he gave them dinner and furnished rations for their horses. The Rebels were subsequently "well cared for."

Richmond Dispatch, April 5, 1896.

**

A colonel in the Texas Brigade was bragging to the locals along the line of march about his men's virtues and finer qualities. Just then, one of his men passed by, toting a large turkey slung over one shoulder. The embarrassed officer called out, "Where did you get that turkey?" Without breaking stride, the soldier replied, "Stole it, sir." The colonel seized on the opportunity, turned to the civilian, and uttered, "Ah, as you see, my boys may steal, but they don't lie."

Harold B. Simpson, Hood's Texas Brigade: Lee's Grenadier Guard. (Waco, Texas: Texian Press, 1970).

**

One member of Crenshaw's Battery marveled at the welcome reception the Virginia artillerymen received as they rumbled through Hagerstown, Maryland. Private John C. Goolsby recorded, "We had the pleasure of seeing numerous Confederate flags displayed, which the boys greeted with loud bursts of applause." The men were pleased with the Southern patriotism, but the real prize still awaited—the bountiful larders of the Keystone State. He continued, "After camping awhile near the town, we broke camp and soon struck the Little Antietam stream, crossed it, and were soon in the land of milk and apple butter—Pennsylvania. What a sight greeted our eyes! This is a beautiful country, and we reached it at a season of the year when the whole earth was wrapped in nature's best attire—the velvet green."

John A. Miller, Files of the Emmitsburg Area Historical Society.

**

While an entire Confederate corps marched towards Pennsylvania, Federal officials (and much of the civilian population) puzzled over conflicting reports and incomplete information. Military intelligence was sporadic at best, and too often relied upon hearsay accounts of troop movements from locals. On June 17, Major General Hooker's chief of staff, Daniel Butterfield, pleaded with a colleague in Washington, D.C., "Try and hunt up somebody from Pennsylvania who knows something, and has a cool enough head to judge what is the actual state of affairs there with regard to the enemy... We cannot go boggling round until we know what we are going after."

11

Official Records of the War of the Rebellion, Vol. 27, Part 3. U.S. Government Printing Office.

**

Even the man most responsible for gathering, analyzing, and initially interpreting intelligence reports in the field was confused in his initial assessment of Lee's intentions. Major General Alfred Pleasonton commanded the cavalry of the Army of the Potomac. After several days trying unsuccessfully to penetrate J.E.B. Stuart's cavalry screen in a series of small battles in the Loudoun Valley, Pleasonton formed his opinion about Confederate objectives from rumors, inadequate scouting, and outdated enemy newspapers, not exactly reliable sources of information on which to base military strategy.

He wrote, "The raid into Pennsylvania appears to be a fizzle & some of the negroes say it is reported Gen. Lee is moving his troops back toward Culpepper [Culpeper Court House]— at any rate the valley between this & the Blue Ridge has no rebel infantry in it as far as I have been able to find out… From this I begin to think the whole business on the part of the rebels has been a grand dodge to be able to send reinforcements to Vicksburg from their army here. I am confirmed in this by a rebel newspaper from Richmond captured yesterday which intimates that their whole success in the rebellion depends upon Vicksburg & it must be saved, & that it will be. Tell the President this…"

The veteran general was wrong; it was not a fizzle. Just beyond the scenic Blue Ridge Mountains, only a few miles away, lurked the bulk of Lee's army, inexorably marching towards Pennsylvania. War was coming to the heartland of the North.

Files of the Library of the Gettysburg National Military Park.

**

The night of June 20 was stormy and wet, and cavalrymen in Virginia's Loudoun Valley from both armies were drenched, including pickets of William "Grumble" Jones's Laurel Brigade, a celebrated Confederate command from the mountains of what had since become West Virginia. Captain Albert Swindler of the 10th Virginia Cavalry collected empty canteens from pickets posted at the Pot House, a crossroads country tavern near Middleburg. After Swindler returned and distributed the canteens, Captain Charles O'Ferrall of the 12th Virginia Cavalry was delighted to find that his now contained "mountain dew," a local form of moonshine. O'Ferrall drank some and reported it was "pretty stimulating." He shared the brew with some of his men, and the ride through the valley to Upperville was much happier.

O'Ferrall and a friend, Lieutenant Walter Buck of the 7th Virginia Cavalry, rode together. They expressed a mutual desire to receive slight wounds in the next skirmish so they could slip home on medical leave and see their families and friends. Buck wanted to be shot in the legs, so his arms would still be free to embrace the pretty girls he expected would greet him. O'Ferrall instead wanted to be wounded in the arm, so he could readily escape, if necessary, from the Union countryside where his house was located. Little did the jovial cavaliers realize they would indeed be shot during the subsequent fighting in the late afternoon at Upperville. Buck was killed and O'Ferrall grievously wounded, somehow eventually recovering from a Yankee carbine shot that lodged in his chest.

Charles T. O'Ferrall, Four Years of Service. (New York and Washington: The Neale Publishing Company, 1904).

**

The Army of the Potomac continued streaming northward to intercept Lee. On June 21, some infantrymen from the Second Corps found an intact artillery shell. Curious about how it worked, they took it to the nearby camp of Battery B, 1st Rhode Island Artillery. One crewman, John F. Tyng, took special delight in presenting himself as an expert on artillery matters. He lifted the shell in his hand and began to explain its peculiarities. About fifty men gathered to hear his passionate discourse on the intricacies of artillery shells. He informed the rapt listeners that it was perfectly safe because it had no percussion fuse.

To show what was inside the shell, he decided to crack it open. Repeated whacks with a sledge hammer failed to break it, and several men took turns hammering on the iron shell. Finally, it started to crack, and Tyng commented that a couple more solid hits should do the trick. A big fellow from the 1st Minnesota Infantry picked up the sledge and gave the shell a tremendous blow. Tyng was wrong; it was a live round. The resulting explosion flung the sledge hammer over one hundred feet into the air, and flying shell fragments broke limbs off a large oak tree above the startled soldiers. Gunners and foot-soldiers alike raced for cover. Amazingly, no one was injured. A chagrined Tyng had gunpowder blown into his face, but he was okay, as were nearby artillery horses.

Thomas M. Aldrich, The History of Battery A, First Regiment Rhode Island Light Artillery in the War to Preserve the Union 1861-1865. (Providence: Snow & Farnham, 1904).

**

As late as June 22, many thought Lee's incursion was merely a grand diversion to shift Union attention from the Western Theater. York, Pennsylvania, attorney James Latimer mentioned the prevailing attitude to his brother, "Either the people of Harrisburg are scared very badly about nothing and are making fools of themselves, or there is some considerable danger to be apprehended. Still many people here say it is nothing but a causeless fright among railroad men." Latimer, skeptical it was a mere sham, traveled to Harrisburg to see Governor Andrew Curtin, receiving chilling assurances that this was no mere "causeless fright"—the Rebels really were coming to Pennsylvania.

James W. Latimer letter to Bartow Latimer, June 18, 1863. Files of the York County Heritage Trust.

**

Both armies relied upon networks of "scouts," intelligence agents who used observation and subterfuge to collect information to be passed along to the generals. The Globe Inn in downtown Gettysburg was opened in 1798 by James Gettys, the founder and namesake of the town. For weeks before the Confederate invasion, owner Charles Wills suspected that certain frequent guests were Southern spies. His tavern was headquarters for the Adams County Democratic Party and became a favorite watering hole for local "Copperheads" (people with strong anti-war sentiments). On June 26, as Rebels occupied town, he recognized one of Major General Jubal Early's aides as a former patron who, just three weeks before, paid for his dinner with a silver quarter.

Gettysburg Compiler, April 24, 1907.
Charles Wills account, Library of the Gettysburg National Military Park

**

Confederate stragglers often provided more reliable information than the scouts. Their identities and military units confirmed the movements of Lee's army in Maryland and Pennsylvania. Roving patrols of Federal militia cavalry rounded up these Rebels and escorted them to Harrisburg for debriefing and processing. There, the new captives joined prisoners incarcerated after previous battles. New Union recruits marveled at their first sight of Southern soldiers. Lieutenant Francis B. Wallace, a Pottsville, Pennsylvania, newspaperman, joined the emergency militia in mid-June and traveled to Camp Curtin in Harrisburg to be trained as a soldier. He reported, "We have had several Rebel prisoners, and one suspected of being a spy, in the guard house here. They are the most forlorn and God-forsaken looking creatures I ever saw—ragged, dirty and lousy; they have little or nothing to say; but nevertheless, seem to be perfectly contented with their situation."

Wallace informed his readers, "Camp life is not altogether devoid of amusements. There is one kind which was quite common in Camp Curtin—a man would get into a blanket, held by fifteen or twenty men, and they would throw him up into the air fifteen or twenty feet. The man while in the air would turn about in all manner of shapes, reminding a person of an acrobat in some circus. He is caught in the blanket again as he comes down."

He added, "On Saturday we received our shelter tents, preparatory for marching. On the inside of mine was written, 'The soldier who gets this tent, will please write to Jessie Wilson, 1302 Ogden street, Philadelphia.' It is unnecessary to assure you that I cheerfully complied with the young lady's request."

Pottsville Miner's Journal, June 27, 1863

Getting a good night's rest was critical to both armies as the days of marching dragged on. The 76th New York had no such luck as it camped near Barnesville, Maryland, on June 25 following a day of intense rain. The regiment was stationed in a flooded cornfield, with water three to six inches deep between the corn rows. Men miserably tried to sleep on saturated blankets spread across mud puddles. Officers placed a strong guard around the cornfield to prevent men from slipping away during the night, but, by morning, the sympathetic guards had allowed most of the men to head across the road to a dry knoll and sleep in a woodlot.

Not far away, Major General James Wadsworth, one of the country's wealthiest men, purchased a large supply of straw for much of his division. When the 76th broke camp at 9 a.m., the men squeezed as much water and muck out of their blankets as possible, rolled them up, and slung them over their shoulders. Lieutenant Abram Smith commented that the blankets were now three times their usual weight. The regiment slogged another sixteen miles in the rain and mud before camping again on soggy ground at Jefferson, Maryland.

Abram P. Smith, History of the Seventy-sixth Regiment, New York Volunteers. (Cortland, New York: Truair, Smith and Miles, 1867)

**

Many Confederates considered the march through lush Pennsylvania to be a great lark—a cornucopia of fresh food, new clothing, spirited music, bountiful supplies, and interesting new sights. Virginia cavalryman James Hodam thought the countryside toward Gettysburg abounded "chiefly in Dutch women who could not speak English, sweet cherries, and apple-butter."

James H. Hodam manuscript, quoted in Brian Kesterson's Campaigning with the 17th Virginia Cavalry, Night Hawks at Monocacy. (Charleston, West Virginia: Night Hawk Press, 2004).

**

Chambersburg newspaperman Alexander McClure was amused by one Confederate stereotype about Pennsylvanians. "Many requisitions were made by Ewell upon the citizens of Chambersburg, all of which were impossible of fulfillment, as all valuables that could be removed had been sent away. One of the most amusing features of his several requisitions was a demand for the immediate delivery of nine barrels of sauerkraut. He knew that sauerkraut was regarded as a very valuable antiscorbutic, and as some of his troop suffered from scurvy because of their unwholesome rations, he assumed that sauerkraut would be an invaluable remedy for those who were threatened with that malady.

He was quite incredulous at first, when informed that sauerkraut was a commodity that could not be kept in midsummer, and that such a thing was unknown even in the German communities where sauerkraut was one of the great staples of the table. If there had been a barrel of sauerkraut in Chambersburg in midsummer he could have scented it any place within a square mile, and he finally abandoned that feature of the requisition when told that it was not an article that could be concealed in hot weather."

Alexander K. McClure, Maneuvering for the Battle, Old Time Notes of Pennsylvania, Vol. II, Chapter LX, 1905.

**

An angry farmer approached a Confederate colonel and complained that a soldier from the Texas Brigade shot his hog. The officer asked if the farmer had heard the gunshot and the pig's subsequent squeal. The farmer confirmed that he indeed heard both the shot and squeal. The colonel stared at him and remarked, "Well, you are in the wrong camp, mister, that I am sure." The farmer had a puzzled look on his face, but the colonel continued, "…for when a Texan shoots a hog, he don't squeal."

Harold B. Simpson, Hood's Texas Brigade: Lee's Grenadier Guard. (Waco, Texas: Texian Press, 1970).

**

Many Marylanders and Pennsylvanians abandoned their homes to take livestock and valuables to safety. The 31st Georgia halted and rested near one such vacated farm. Confederates entered the yard to pick ripe cherries and, fearing they might be tempted to create additional mischief, Colonel Clement Evans kept an eye on them. He found his men in the rear of the farmhouse near an underground milk and butter house. Evans was relieved they had not touched anything, although the door was unlocked, and the soldiers knew the cellar was well stocked. More worrisome than milk was the availability of alcohol. The colonel reflected that "the citizens supply our troops too liberally with whiskey—surely they can ruin our army by a liberality of that sort unless the orders are enforced."

Clement Evans' diary entry, June 23, 1863.

**

As Nathaniel Smith and his comrades in the 13th North Carolina approached Chambersburg, they marched by a farmhouse, "in front of which an old Dutch woman, fat and lusty, sat rocking herself vigorously in an arm-chair. The band of the Thirteenth Regiment was playing 'Maryland, My Maryland.' On the completion of the tune, the old lady arose and in her broken English screamed at the top of her voice: 'Oh, yes! Oh, yes! It's 'Maryland, My Maryland' but when you come back it will be 'Fire in the mountains; run, boys, run!'" [another popular song in those days]. An amused Smith added, "...and with a hoarse, loud laugh, she resumed her seat and rocked more vigorously than ever."

Walter Clark, Histories of the Several Regiments and Battalions from North Carolina in the Great War 1861-1865. Volume 1 (Raleigh, North Carolina: E. M. Uzzell, 1901).

**

On June 26, Major General Jubal Early's Confederates easily chased away hastily recruited Pennsylvania emergency militia guarding Gettysburg. The veteran Rebels captured 175 frightened Yankees, mostly boys and young men who mustered into the service just three days earlier at Harrisburg's Camp Curtin. Confederates roamed Gettysburg's streets, stealing horses and liberating stashes of liquor. They sent wagonloads of supplies and herds of livestock back to Virginia. As Rebels fanned out south of town, cavalrymen encountered a pair of Union militiamen from the local Adams County Cavalry. Shots rang out, and twenty-year-old George Washington Sandoe, a soldier just a few days and a husband only four months, was killed. Local miller and outspoken abolitionist Peter McAllister recovered the body and turned it over to the grieving family for burial. Sandoe was the first of more than 5,000 men who would die within a week at Gettysburg.

Files of the Adams County Historical Society.

**

Confederate patrols rounded up Pennsylvanians suspected of being Federal employees, including the postmasters of the villages of Greenmount (south of Gettysburg) and Fairfield (formerly Millerstown, in Adams County southwest of Gettysburg). They seized a few innocent farmers and townspeople, accusing them of being spies.

Among these captives was 57-year-old George J. Codori, a Gettysburg carriage maker who lived on Middle Street. Rebel cavalry seized him while he was returning from Baltimore after delivering a buggy to a client. He was driving a wagon and wearing standard Federal-issue light blue army pants, perhaps a gift sent home by his son Nicolas, a soldier in a Pennsylvania regiment. The Rebels may have thought he was a Union teamster. For two years, the Confederate army detained Codori and other civilians at various prison camps throughout the South. Unfortunately, one Pennsylvanian died in prison shortly after being transported from Gettysburg. George Codori was finally released in March 1865. Weakened by exposure and pneumonia, he managed to return home to Gettysburg. However, his tear-filled reunion was short-lived, as he died three days later. He was buried in St. Francis Xavier Catholic Cemetery.

Files of the Adams County Historical Society.
Gary Kross, Attack from the West, Blue & Gray, Volume XVII, Issue 5.

**

Most Pennsylvanians did not know what to make of the invaders. Stories of robbery and vandalism spread, as did reports of drunkenness and debauchery. Contrasting accounts told of Southern hospitality and consideration extended to civilians. Confederate adjutant Randolph McKim later wrote, "At Springfield I bought seven copies of the New Testament for distribution among the men. The surprise of the storekeeper when an officer of the terrible Rebel Army desired to purchase copies of the New Testament may be imagined. Perhaps he thought if the rebels would read the Good Book, they might repent of their wicked Rebellion."

Randolph H. McKim, A Soldier's Recollections: Leaves from the Diary of a Young Confederate. (New York: Longmans, Green, and Co., 1910).

**

Foragers from the 35th Battalion, Virginia Cavalry spotted a country store near Porters Sideling in southwestern York County. Storekeeper Aaron Rudisill was sitting on a cracker barrel when Rebels entered his store. Startled, he fell into the huge barrel and became stuck. With only his head and feet showing, an officer tilted the barrel onto its side. Young Rudisill, trapped in the barrel, sat dumbfounded on the floor while the soldiers cleaned him out, leaving behind a few Confederate bills as a token payment. Rudisill's father, John, was a draft dodger. He spent the summer hiding in a cave to avoid conscription because he lacked enough money to pay the $300 bounty for a substitute. Another son, William, brought him food each day.

Armand Glatfelter, The Flowering of the North Codorus Palatinate: A History of North Codorus Township. (York, Pennsylvania: Mehl, 1988).

**

Spies for both armies were active in southern Pennsylvania before and during the invasion. Emanating from civil and military leaders in Chambersburg and Gettysburg, scouts carried secret messages written on tissue paper stuffed in their pockets, where they could be quickly fingered into a little ball and swallowed in case of capture. Likewise, the Rebels had their own spy network. Both sides sought to capture these couriers, as well as others suspected of covert activities. The provost squad of the 31st Georgia passed through

Abbottstown, a turnpike rest stop east of Gettysburg near the border of Adams and York counties. They sought out John Wolf, a Federal army recruiting agent and vocal opponent of secret pro-secessionist "Copperhead" organizations. Informants asked the Rebels to take him prisoner, but Wolf received sufficient warning to escape from Abbottstown prior to their arrival. He was a relative of 94-year-old Jacob Wolf, patriarch of a massive clan that included five generations of his 240 direct descendents. The elderly Wolf had remained home while the Rebels passed through town. He lived to be 100, dying in March 1869.

History of Cumberland and Adams Counties, Pennsylvania. (Chicago: Warner, Beers & Co., 1886).

**

On June 27, Lieutenant Colonel Elijah White's Rebel cavalrymen visited Hanover, a bustling railroad town in southwestern York County. They procured horses, food, liquor, supplies, and personal items, usually paying in worthless Confederate scrip. A number of merchants and shopkeepers had taken their most valuable merchandise into hiding. However, some procrastinators were still in town when White's men rode into the center square. Jeweler William Boadenhamer, after a late start, was frantically leaving Hanover on the York Road. Gun-toting cavalrymen overtook his carriage about a mile from town and stole a large box of retail goods. Resting under a shade tree near a grist mill, they opened the chest and discovered it contained nearly one hundred watches and jewelry pieces. They distributed part of the loot among themselves. Later that day, a soldier gave a stolen brooch to a little girl he encountered in Jefferson. It is one of the few jewelry pieces known to have been recovered from the entire haul. What happened to the rest?

In a 1906 letter, White informed former cavalry officer John S. Mosby that, on his way to sacking the railroad depot at Hanover Junction, "Nothing occurred on the way of any consequence, except I captured a wagon load of jewelry. After supplying ourselves, we buried the balance." White's buried treasure may still be stuck underground somewhere along Oil Creek east of Hanover.

George R. Prowell, History of York County, Pennsylvania. (Chicago: J. H. Beers and Co., 1907).
John S. Mosby, Stuart's Cavalry in the Gettysburg Campaign. (New York: Moffat, Yard & Company, 1908).

**

Confederate horsemen under Brigadier General Albert G. Jenkins, a former Democratic U.S. Congressman from western Virginia, raided farms for horses, livestock, and other items of interest to the mountaineers. Jenkins departed Carlisle on Sunday, June 28, with 250 soldiers and rode from Mechanicsburg toward northwestern York County, intent on visiting prosperous Dillsburg. Near the hamlet of Williams Grove, his men spotted a large, brightly colored U.S. flag waving atop a nearby low mountain. Entering the village, General Jenkins encountered a civilian named Lee Welty, who lied and calmly informed the

Virginian that the banner marked the vanguard of the oncoming Union Army. Jenkins halted his advance and splashed back across Yellow Breeches Creek to regroup. The flag was a ruse, having been planted on the mountaintop by local boys. Dillsburg residents used this brief respite to hide their valuables and horses in nearby woods. Hotelkeepers stashed their liquor, and pharmacist George Shearer secreted his wooden barrel of "medicinal whiskey" in his barn. After Jenkins figured out there were no Yankees in the area, he occupied Dillsburg, but found little to procure except forage and food.

George R. Prowell, History of York County, Pennsylvania. (Chicago: J. H. Beers and Co., 1907).

**

Near the village of Fairfield, Rebel artillerymen from Virginia and South Carolina were searching for horses suitable for use as draft animals. One squad from the Pee Dee Artillery approached an old brick farmhouse, its doors shut and blinds tightly closed. The only sign of life was a broken-down blind bay horse tethered in a nearby orchard. It was clearly not acceptable for artillery usage. However, a couple of soldiers thought they had seen a different horse, one that appeared healthy, being led through a gate towards the house. They concluded that it must be hidden within the house.

The Confederates repeatedly knocked on the door. Finally, a pale and badly frightened woman opened it. Sergeant Joseph Brunson, in charge of the squad, assured her "they would not hurt a hair on her head." He inquired about the horse spotted at her gate and offered to buy it for military duty. She responded, "I have no horse but that one in the orchard. You can take him if you want to." The Southerners did not want the blind nag and insisted they saw another horse, which now must be in the house. Distressed by their insistence on inspecting her home, the woman replied, "If you men come into the house, you will scare my poor crazy sister to death."

Brunson instructed his squad to stay outside and then followed the woman into a long hallway. Two doors opened on either side, with a single one at the far end. She readily opened the side doors and remarked, "You see no horse is here." Brunson pointed to the remaining door and mentioned she had not opened that one. She exclaimed, "Surely you would not go into a lady's bedroom." An exasperated Brunson replied, "By no means, Ma'am, but it is no harm to look in."

The woman relented and cracked open the door, allowing him a quick peek at the opposite wall. Suspicious, he pushed the door fully open. There, he saw a fine bay horse, his feet on a mantilla (a short cape) to deaden the sound of his hooves on the wooden floor. It was apparently a pet, as three little children were sitting on a bed and playing with its mane. The woman rushed forward, threw her arms around the horse's neck, and suddenly screamed out, "You shan't take my dead husband's horse!"

The children screamed in terror, and the crazy sister joined in with a vigor that clearly demonstrated, though her mind was out of order, her lungs and vocal chords were sound. The scene was so pitiful and the racket so disconcerting the veteran sergeant regretted prosecuting the search. He knew that Union troops had perpetrated atrocities upon innocent

Southerners far worse than dragging a pet horse away from screaming youngsters. However, their appealing cries rang in his ears, and their tearful faces evoked compassion. Plus, there was that crazy sister to deal with. Who knew what she was capable of? He also knew his men expected him to emerge with the horse.

Suddenly, he realized how to resolve the problem. He strode back to the front door and told the waiting patrol he found the horse. However, he needed to be sure the animal was suitable for the rigors of military work. Taking a trusted comrade inside, Brunson explained the situation and whispered they <u>had</u> to find something wrong with the horse to justify leaving it behind. His companion inspected the steed and discovered a very small saddle sore on its back. Satisfied, the two men emerged from the house and declared the horse to be sore-backed and totally unfit for artillery duty. The squad mounted and moved on to the next farm, leaving the grateful children still in the bedroom clutching their pet.

Joseph W. Brunson, Cannoneers as Cavalrymen, Recollections and Reminiscences, 1861-1865. Volume 6. (Florence: South Carolina Division of the United Daughters of the Confederacy; based on an undated manuscript).

**

A York County family tried a similar trick, only with much different results. They had secreted a fine draft horse in their elegant parlor. When a patrol of the feared "Louisiana Tigers stopped at the front door, the residents denied having a horse. However, it neighing confirmed its presence. Confederates barged inside, seized the frightened animal from beside an expensive rosewood piano, and led it away. The farmer was left with a fistful of worthless Confederate currency and a parlor that smelled like a barnyard.

William J. Seymour, A Louisiana Tiger: The Civil War Memoirs of Captain William J. Seymour, manuscript copy in the Library of the Gettysburg National Military Park.

**

Residents often took drastic measures, including secreting horses and mules in houses and straw sheds, dropping sacks of silverware and valuables down wells to be fished out later, and temporarily hobbling horses to make them appear lame and useless to the Confederates. At one farm, several fine draft horses were concealed under a large apple tree with branches that hung to the ground, providing good cover. The animals were gagged, and a farmer used a fly brush to keep them from stomping their feet and attracting attention. In another case, an old lady smeared soft cow dung on her horse. Raiders laughed and passed over the foul-smelling animal.

Ronald L. Botterbusch, Civil War Hours in Dover Township – When Confederates Passed Through, A History of Dover Township, York County, Pennsylvania: 1790s–1990s. (Dover, Pa.: Dover Township Board of Supervisors, 1994).

**

Confidence abounded in Lee's army, as his soldiers rarely had tasted defeat. As they tramped through Maryland and Pennsylvania, most were certain another victory loomed, and Southern battle flags would be waving soon in the streets of some of the North's most prominent cities. Few thought they could be stopped. On June 28, the 17th Virginia Cavalry rode eastward through York County to burn a pair of large railroad bridges at the mouth of Conewago Creek. They paused in the villages of Manchester and Mount Wolf, where soldiers shopped for boots, shoes, hats, and clothing. They paid their bills in Confederate currency, which they proudly affirmed soon would be "better than your greenbacks, as we are now on our way to Harrisburg, Philadelphia, and New York, and the war will soon be over."

George R. Prowell, History of York County, Pennsylvania. (Chicago: J. H. Beers and Co., 1907).

**

Rebels passed through Greencastle and demanded gunpowder, bullets, vegetables, and whatever else their army could use. The town had no supplies of munitions, but several crates of vegetables were delivered to the sidewalk at the Hollar Hotel. Townsman John Reid was at Rowe's general store when he spotted a neighbor, Mr. Miller, whose son had been killed by lightning in the spring of 1862. Miller walked alone down the street, carrying a fine saddle and bridle he had bought for his son before his untimely death. Reid asked him where he was going with the saddle and bridle. Miller replied, "Hollar Hotel, to deliver them to the Rebels' requisition." A concerned Reid inquired, "Mr. Miller, have you got an ordinary saddle and bridle? This one is too good to give to the Johnnies." He responded. "I have an old one, but if the rebels searched and found this new saddle, they might burn my property." He walked over to the hotel and gave the new saddle and bridle to the enemy soldiers, his fear taking precedence over his sentimental (and financial) attachment to his dead son's property.

John W. P. Reid, Recollections of Lee's Invasion, Kauffman's Progressive News, April 11, 1919.

**

Confederates occupied Chambersburg for several days, confiscating food supplies and equipment of value to the army. They forced local grist mills to continue to operate to supply fresh ground flour for the hungry soldiers. Residents soon looked to the surrounding country for daily supplies of flour, vegetables and meats. Yet, because most draft teams had been sent away to safety and Rebels now ringed the town, no relief supplies could be brought in. Within a few days, townspeople grew hungry. Mrs. William McLellan, the wife of a leading attorney, visited General Lee's headquarters in Shetter's woods, not far from her residence. Promptly admitted to his presence, she appealed to him to permit supplies to be brought into town without being seized by his army. A compassionate Lee arranged to have sufficient supplies of flour furnished to the townspeople.

After Lee's generous orders were transmitted, Mrs. McLellan thanked him and asked him for his autograph, to which he replied: "Do you want the autograph of a rebel?" She replied, "General Lee, I am a true Union woman and yet I ask for bread and for your autograph." He answered, "It is to your interest to be for the Union and I hope you may be as firm in your purpose as I am in mine." Lee gave her the autograph, and Mrs. McLellan brought bread to her starving neighbors. Among her most cherished relics during her later life was her autograph of Robert E. Lee.

Alexander K. McClure, Maneuvering for the Battle, Old Time Notes of Pennsylvania, Vol. II, Chapter LX, 1905.

**

The Army of the Potomac marched steadily northward through Maryland in pursuit of Lee's army. Just outside of Frederick, men from the 14th Vermont broke ranks and began to climb nearby cherry trees. Soon, there appeared to be more soldiers in the trees than cherries. Brigadier General George Stannard, perhaps concerned over the ramification unripe cherries might have on his men's constitutions, sent an orderly to hustle the soldiers back into column. They ignored him and kept gorging. Stannard, frustrated his orders were not obeyed, then sent a staff officer. The infantrymen climbed down from the trees and reformed. The officer, satisfied his authority had generated results, smugly rode off. As soon as he was out of sight, the Vermonters scrambled back up into the trees and resumed munching the cherries. General Stannard, by now thoroughly upset, rode over to the orchard and took personal charge of getting his men back on the road to Frederick. His only recorded words were, "Lord bless your souls, get out of the cherry trees." Doubtless, he used much more colorful language, for Stannard was known for his sharp tongue.

George G. Benedict, A Short History of the 14th Vermont Reg't. (Bennington, Vermont: C.A. Pierce, 1887).

**

As one Union brigade was marching through a town, the drum corps struck up lively music. The colonel noticed that one drummer boy was not beating his drum. He asked his adjutant to find out why the boy was not playing. Riding up to the musicians, the adjutant, with a deep frown on his face, shouted at the boy, "The colonel wants to know why you are not beating your drum?" In a whisper loud enough to be enjoyed some distance down the line, the culprit replied, "Tell the colonel that I can't beat my drum now. I have two live turkeys in my drum—and one of them is for the colonel!"

Henry M. Kieffer, Recollections of a Drummer Boy. (Boston: Ticknor and Co., 1889).

**

Captain John A. Lonergan of the 13th Vermont was a native of County Tipperary in Ireland. The hard-drinking, irrepressible Irishman tumbled off his horse while fording the Monocacy River near Frederick. He was sober at the time, and his men laughed that he simply took a much needed bath. The soggy officer responded, "Too much liquid on the outside, and not enough on the inside, or it would not have happened." The fun-loving Lonergan would be awarded the Medal of Honor for his actions at Gettysburg on July 2.

John Lonergan File, National Archives and Records Administration.

**

Alcohol caused much consternation after the main Union force passed through Frederick. Correspondent Whitelaw Reid sent the Cincinnati *Gazette* this description, "Frederick is Pandemonium. Somebody has blundered frightfully; the town is full of stragglers, and the liquor-shops are in full blast. Just under my window, scores of drunken soldiers are making night hideous; all over the town they are trying to steal horses, or sneak into unwatched private residences, or are filling the air with the blasphemy of their drunken brawls. The worst elements of a great army are here in their worst condition; its cowards, its thieves, its sneaks, its bullying vagabonds, all inflamed with whiskey, and drunk as well with their freedom from accustomed restraint."

Frank Moore, The Rebellion Record: A Diary of American Events. Volume VII. (New York: D. Van Nostrand, 1864).

**

Residents had mixed feelings towards the Federal soldiers. Many openly welcomed them and fed them, or shared supplies and cold drinks. Others charged high prices for food and refreshments, much to the chagrin of the passing soldiers. North of Frederick, the Fifth Corps passed through the town of Liberty. A farmer rode into the village, the contents of his wagon concealed by several white tablecloths. Soldiers crowded around him. One, lifting the corner of a cloth remarked, "What have ye got to sell, old fellow? Bread eh?" The wagon was loaded with dozens of large loaves of fresh soft bread and several bushels of ginger cakes. "What do you ask for a loaf?" the soldier inquired.

"I haven't any to sell," replied the farmer. "Haven't any to sell? What are ye here for?" asked the impudent soldier, to which he received no reply from the farmer. "See here, old fellow, won't ye sell me a hunk of your gingerbread?" "No," came the soft reply from the farmer.

The soldier erupted in anger, "Well, you are a mean old cuss. It would be serving you right to tip you out of your old bread-cart. Here we are marching all night and all day to protect your property, and fight the rebs. We haven't had any breakfast, and may not have any dinner. You are a set of mean cusses around here, I reckon."

The heated exchange drew a crowd of soldiers, some of whom also expressed indignation that the man would not sell them any bread or ginger cakes. The old farmer took it all in, and then stood up from his wagon seat. He took off the tablecloths, revealing the full extent of his array of delicacies. He looked at the accusers and calmly remarked, "I didn't bring my bread here to sell. My wife and daughters set up all night to bake it for you, and you are welcome to all I've got, and wish I had ten times as much." His next words struck like a thunderbolt to the suddenly silent crowd, "Help yourselves, boys."

The stunned and chagrined soldiers now appreciated his compassionate intentions and erupted in praise, "Hurrah! Hurrah! Hurrah!" "Bully for you!" "You're a brick!" "Three cheers for the old man!" "Three more for the old woman!" and "Three more for the girls!" The soldiers threw their caps in the air and danced with joy in celebration of the Maryland family's generosity. The bread and cakes were gone in a twinkling as men scrambled to empty the wagon. The farmer prepared to return home and sat down on his wagon seat. The once impudent soldier walked up to the farmer, extended his hand, and apologized for his rudeness, "See here, my friend, I take back all the hard words I said about you." Overcome with emotion, the farmer clasped the soldier's hand. All was forgiven.

Charles Carleton Coffin, The Boys of 61, or Four Years of Fighting: Personal Observation With the Army and Navy. (Boston: The Page Company, 1896).

**

On Sunday, June 28, while Confederates roamed throughout York, Cumberland, and Franklin counties, Gettysburg, in adjoining Adams County, was now free of Rebels. About noon, two regiments of finely equipped Michigan cavalry rode northward from Emmitsburg, Maryland, into the borough, the first troops from the Army of the Potomac to arrive. Residents rejoiced, relieved that safety was at hand, and several presented flowers to soldiers. A few lucky men enjoyed kisses from Gettysburg's maidens. Townspeople distributed pitchers and buckets of cold, refreshing water and milk. With the emergency apparently over and Jubal Early's troops now far off in York, citizens uncovered their hidden stores. Laughing and singing, many began cooking and feeding their welcome friends in blue uniforms. Supplies of liquor emerged to be shared with the troopers, and a festive atmosphere pervaded the town. Little did the residents or soldiers realize the magnitude of the unspeakable horrors awaiting them in the upcoming week.

History of Cumberland and Adams Counties, Pennsylvania. (Chicago: Warner, Beers & Co., 1886).

**

That Sunday evening, eighteen Confederates rode into a churchyard outside Fairfield. Lieutenant John Chamberlayne of the Crenshaw Artillery pointed a pistol at the parishioners while his Virginians unhitched their horses. He gave each owner a voucher for repayment upon a peace treaty between the Confederacy and the United States. Not long afterwards, a Federal cavalry patrol captured Chamberlayne and some of his men and recovered the stolen horses.

Gettysburg Compiler, June 29, 1863.
G.C. Chamberlayne, Ham Chamberlayne – Virginian. (Richmond: The Thetz Printing Company, 1932).

**

A spy informed Lee about a recent change in command of the Federal Army of the Potomac—Major General George Meade had replaced "Fighting Joe" Hooker. Perhaps of more immediate interest to Lee, the scout placed the Union army much closer to the Confederates than Lee envisioned. He ordered his scattered detachments to rendezvous. Chambersburg officials became convinced that the rapid movement of troops, artillery, and supply trains eastward from there meant Lee's army no longer targeted Harrisburg, but instead was concentrating near Gettysburg. They wanted to communicate this vital information to Governor Andrew Curtin, but all nearby telegraph lines were severed. The fastest way remaining to transmit this news to Curtin was for a courier to travel through enemy-held territory to the nearest operational telegraph station, well to the north along the Pennsylvania Railroad.

Judge F. M. Kimmel, acting as the head of Chambersburg's civil government, wrote a succinct summary of local military affairs, stressing the Rebels' hurried departure eastward towards Gettysburg. He entrusted the message to a reliable scout, former Union soldier Stephen Pomeroy, whose father had been his associate judge. The note was sewn securely into lining of the buckle strap on Pomeroy's pants. The judge informed him the message was of great importance to the country, "Get this safe and in the shortest time to the governor."

Pomeroy traveled doggedly along back roads northward, changing horses frequently and taking off-road short cuts over hills and through ravines, fields, and woods. He crossed over the mountains and, after walking seventeen and riding forty-one miles, arrived at Port Royal in Juniata County well after midnight. He entered the telegraph station and informed the operator of the hidden message. It was taken from his pants lining and quickly wired to the governor. By 4:00 a.m., the news had been relayed to Washington and forwarded to

Major General Meade. Troops were set in motion to investigate the report. Years later, Andrew Curtin sent a belated thank-you note to Pomeroy, who was now a respected preacher, a drastic change from his days as a secret agent.

Samuel P. Bates and Richard J. Fraise. History of Franklin County, Pennsylvania. (Chicago: Warner, Beers and Co., 1887).
Alexander K. McClure, Lee Defeated At Gettysburg, Old Time Notes of Pennsylvania, Vol. II, Chapter LXI (Chambersburg, Pennsylvania: 1905).

**

Jubal Early's Confederates occupied York June 28 and 29. Soldiers visited old acquaintances, relaxed, cleaned equipment, and foraged for supplies. One York clothing merchant had concealed most of his inventory. An officer from the Louisiana Tigers knocked on the door, and the old man responded that he had nothing left to sell. The Confederate offered gold for some fresh shirts, and the storekeeper opened his store and allowed the Rebel to select what he wanted. The Southerner returned to his quarters and declared to his men where they could obtain shirts. The Tigers headed into downtown York, stopped at the old man's store and asked for shirts. The merchant refused to sell any to them, so the Rebels pushed him aside and entered the store to check for themselves. They found the shirts, as well as a supply of aged whiskey and other choice liquors.

When he refused to give them any alcohol, the Tigers locked him out of his store and proceeded to "indulge in a great spree." Soon, a crowd of onlookers huddled outside his windows, peering in at the commotion inside. The soldiers, perhaps more honest than the shopkeeper feared, emerged with their arms loaded with large quantities of merchandise. They asked him to tally up the bill so they could pay for their selections. They handed him CSA currency, leaving him with a "rueful countenance," notwithstanding the assurances of the officers that the day would come when he would be *glad* to have some Confederate money in his possession.

John A. Gibson, History of York County, Pennsylvania, with Illustrations. (Chicago: F.A. Battey Publishing Co., 1886).

**

War brings out all sorts of emotions in the combatants and civilian populace, from fear, hatred, and loathing to compassion, concern, and chivalry. An informal code of honor, left over from preceding generations of "gentleman warriors," considered it cowardly and unfair to shoot a man in the back as he was leaving the scene of battle. In several instances in the Civil War, entire regiments held their fire as beaten opponents withdrew. At other times, officers ordered their men to blaze away. For most soldiers, however, pulling the trigger at a retreating foe was a highly personal decision. One incident from the Battle of Westminster, a cavalry fight two days before Gettysburg, perhaps illustrates best how soldiers often formulated their own rules of engagement.

On June 29, a reconnaissance patrol from the 4th Virginia Cavalry, in advance of J.E.B. Stuart's main force, approached the northern Maryland village of Westminster. The Southerners were surprised by a courageous charge by a part of the 1st Delaware Cavalry. Fighting intensified as more Confederates arrived and, for the badly outnumbered Yankees, it soon became every man for himself. One retreating Union trooper galloped down Main Street, with a Rebel in hot pursuit. The Confederate steadily closed the distance and finally drew beside the Yankee. He placed his revolver on his target's back and squeezed the trigger. The lining of the Federal's coat flew open from the blast, and the stricken man slumped forward on his horse. Townspeople later recovered his body in a nearby barn.

Files of the Carroll County Historical Society, Westminster, Maryland.

**

Residents near the Mason-Dixon Line had mixed loyalties during the Civil War. Two Westminster brothers were arrested in the summer of 1862 and accused of harboring Confederate sentiments and leading secessionist activities in the area. They hastily left town, headed southward into Virginia, and signed up for the Rebel army. Ironically, they fought at Westminster in front of their anguished mother's house on Main Street.

Files of the Carroll County Historical Society, Westminster, Maryland.

**

Eight miles from Waynesboro, the 17th Pennsylvania Cavalry camped for the evening of June 29, happy to be back in the Keystone State. They entered the commonwealth earlier in the afternoon, passing by their color bearer, who sat on his horse astride the Mason-Dixon Line designating the border between Maryland and Pennsylvania. The boys doffed their caps and loudly cheered Old Glory and their home state. Captain Luther B. Kurtz allowed his Company G to head to their nearby homes for the night for a surprise visit with their families, strictly warning that all men must report back for duty at sunrise. Each man complied, and none was AWOL when the roll was called in the morning.

H. P. Moyer, ed., History of the Seventeenth Regiment Pennsylvania Volunteer Cavalry. (Lebanon, Pennsylvania: Sowers Printing Company, 1911).

**

The Civil War is sometimes called a conflict of "brother against brother." This was true for both the military, where there are hundreds of examples of brothers serving in the opposing armies, and the civilian populace. Perhaps nowhere in America was this more evident than in Union Mills, Maryland, a hamlet consisting of an agricultural-industrial complex and a pair of homesteads owned by two brothers. Part of J.E.B. Stuart's Rebel cavalry camped Monday night, June 29, on the sprawling farm of William Shriver, where they were welcome guests. The next morning, Mrs. Shriver opened her breakfast table to General Stuart and some of his officers and staff. The cavaliers regaled the family with war stories and led choruses of popular Southern songs around a large Steinway piano. Sixteen-year-old son Herbert Shriver volunteered to guide Stuart's column to a back road that led to Hanover, Pennsylvania, bypassing Federal cavalry reportedly in nearby Littlestown. Stuart later used his influence to have the lad enrolled in Virginia Military Institute; young Shriver served in the VMI Cadet Corps at the Battle of New Market in 1864. All five of his brothers also fought in the Confederate army.

Directly across the road from William Shriver's farm was a large grist mill owned by his brother, Andrew, a staunch Unionist and vocal opponent of the Confederate cause. The day after the Rebels left, he entertained Union troops. One of his sons, Henry, was in the emergency Pennsylvania militia defeated by Confederate cavalry on June 26 on the Witmer farm north of Gettysburg. Another son, Louis, later wrote, "Our two families lived close together, and, although we continued to visit back and forth, social intercourse was always strained and often resulted in unhappy arguments."

Files of the Carroll County Historical Society, Westminster, Maryland.

**

The Texas Brigade camped in Chambersburg on June 29. The following morning brought confirmation of the men's legendary status as some of Lee's best foragers. J. B. Polley of the 4th Texas wrote, "Every square foot of an acre of ground not occupied by a sleeping or standing soldier was covered with choice food for the hungry. Chickens, turkeys, duck and geese squawked, gobbled, cackled, quacked, and hissed in harmonious unison as deft and energetic hands seized them for the slaughter and, scarcely waiting for them to die, sent their feathers flying in all directions."

J. B. Polley, Hood's Texas Brigade: Its Marches, Its Battles, Its Achievements. (New York: Neale Publishing Co., 1910).

**

In compliance with Lee's order to concentrate the army, Jubal Early's battle-hardened Confederates reluctantly left York early Tuesday morning, June 30, and retraced their steps westward. A numbers of stragglers and deserters freely roamed the countryside. In a few isolated cases, these "atrocious villains" took out their frustrations on residences abandoned by owners who had taken horses and valuables across the Susquehanna River to safety. Near the railroad and communication center of Hanover Junction in southern York County, vengeful Confederates shattered several windows and entered the locked house of Jacob Smeich. After stealing an accordion, two bonnets, a woolen shawl, and other personal property, they ransacked the house, destroying furniture and smashing glassware, pottery, and Mrs. Smeich's looking glass.

York County Damage Claims, Pennsylvania State Archives, Harrisburg.

**

Pennsylvanians had mixed reactions to the invasion. Refugees choked roads leading north to Harrisburg and east to Columbia, both towns being across the Susquehanna River. Other residents hid horses and mules in the mountains and woods. Some went about their daily business, ignoring the threat. When Rebels actually arrived, some shut their windows and doors and locked themselves in their houses. Others opened their homes and welcomed the Southerners. During the Battle of Hanover on June 30, Samuel Mumma entered his barn and climbed into its spacious hayloft. He spent the day peering from a hole in his roof, watching the distant smoke and occasional movement of cavalry troops. Nearby, he could see Rebels scurrying about the property of his neighbor, Jacob Bart, who scrambled into his cellar for the duration of the fighting. Mumma perhaps had good reason to keep his eye on the Rebels. Three days earlier, Confederate raiders visited his farm and stole one of his horses.

Files of the Hanover Historical Society, Hanover, Pennsylvania.

**

South of Gettysburg, over 90,000 Federal soldiers marched towards an encounter with Robert E. Lee's oft-victorious Confederate army. However, the Yankees' morale was high, and northern Maryland residents eagerly supported the Union cause. For many soldiers, the road to Gettysburg passed through the small seminary town of Emmitsburg. One infantryman later recalled, "Small flags waved and dipped from the tower of the old Lutheran Church, used as a signal station by the army. Bearers of dispatches and squads of cavalry dashed madly through the town. The long roll of drums and the blood-stirring bugle calls filled the air; the fields were alive with soldiers. To the untrained eye, it looked like a great mob....

When the army began to arrive in town, the first thing the soldiers asked for was fresh bread. Nearly every house in the town was turned into a bakery and every woman who could bake was busy day and night, kneading bread while the soldiers needed more. The old-fashioned loaf was about three times bigger than the present baker's loaf. It was interesting to see a soldier, with a loaf under each arm, meet a squad of comrades. He would at once break the bread and hand it around. It would vanish quicker than the morning dew. No doubt it tasted to the poor fellows like the bread mother used to bake at home. The mother and the home that many a brave boy never saw again."

Emmitsburg Chronicle, 1951; cited by John A. Miller, Emmitsburg Area Historical Society.

**

Not far from Emmitsburg, the 76th New York passed by a farmhouse set back over five hundred yards from the crowded road. Wanting to bypass this logjam of troops, Major Andrew Grover decided to cut across the fields. His regiment turned into the farm lane and began marching past the house. The old German farmer, shocked to see soldiers marching on his private property, ran over to the column and began exclaiming, "Dare ish no road up dis way!" The troops kept tramping by, headed for one of his fields. In despair, he addressed every officer that marched by, "My Got, you can't go dis way!" He pleaded, "Tare ish no road up dis way!" By the time the troops had passed by, there was indeed a well-worn road across his fields.

Abram P. Smith, History of the Seventy-sixth Regiment, New York Volunteers. (Cortland, New York: Truair, Smith and Miles, printers, 1867)

**

As Union soldiers camped near Emmitsburg, soldiers purchased all the tobacco in town and bought all the whiskey they could get. One barkeep filled hundreds of canteens at one dollar each until the provost marshal, Captain Schofield, stopped him and placed guards in front of the establishment.

James A. Helman, Helman's History of Emmitsburg, Maryland. (1906).

**

At times, Pennsylvania citizens took matters into their own hands. As Union troops from the Twelfth Corps approached Littlestown, southeast of Gettysburg, cavalry scouts ran into a Confederate picket post. Henry Morhous of the 123rd New York later recalled the valor (and perhaps recklessness) of one civilian, "As the cavalry advance came into Littlestown, one old man volunteered to show them where a squad of Rebel cavalry were. True to his word the old man piloted them right, and soon the cavalry were engaged; but instead of retreating when the fight commenced, the old man went in on his own hook." He dragged one Rebel from his horse, and having no weapons, choked him into submission. The Confederates fled, and the Federal infantry entered Littlestown to cheers and songs from the citizens, who lavished the passing soldiers with cold meats, fresh bread and cakes, and cold water.

Henry C. Morhous, Reminiscences of the 123d Regiment, N.Y.S.V. (Greenwich, New York: People's Journal Book and Job Office, 1879).

**

As he was leaving Hanover following the June 30 cavalry battle, J.E.B. Stuart detained a "fat Dutchman" who was suspiciously counting the Rebel horsemen. The general thought the man was too well informed to be left behind with the enemy and requested that he "come along" on a nearby Conestoga draft horse. Captain John Esten Cook watched as the Pennsylvanian ignored the request. A cavalryman "made a tremendous blow," and the corpulent civilian mounted the massive horse "in hot haste, with only a halter to guide the elephant." Confederates roared with laughter when "the Conestoga ran off, descended the slope at full speed, bounded elephant-like over an enormous ditch—and it was only by clinging close with hands and knees that the Dutchman kept his seat. Altogether, the spectacle was one to tickle the ribs of death." Cooke added, "The last I saw of the captive, he was in the very centre of the cavalry column, which was moving at a trot, and he was swept on with it; passing away for ever from the eyes of this historian, who knows not what became of him thereafter."

John Esten Cooke, Wearing of the Gray, Being Personal Portraits, Scenes & Adventures of the War. (New York: E.B. Treat & Co., 1867)

**

Two brigades of John Buford's cavalry arrived in Gettysburg on June 30, scattering stragglers from Pettigrew's North Carolina brigade. The Federals arrived to the cheers of the citizens, and a group of fifteen to twenty schoolgirls serenaded the 8th Illinois Cavalry with strains of When This Cruel War is Over. According to one trooper, "Many were beautiful, and all were good singers. It seemed to me that they made not the slightest discord, and the sweetest music I ever heard came from their lips…"

Washington Davis, Camp-fire Chats of the Civil War. (Chicago: The Coburn Publishing Company, 1884)

**

Rebel raiders rounded up thousands of horses, cattle, chickens, and other livestock, as well as stealing (or buying with Confederate scrip) forage, food, and provisions. After the war, farmers in the affected counties were encouraged to file damage claims, most of which were never paid. However, these legal documents offer a glimpse of the extent of the losses experienced by the residents. One prominent miller near Hanover, William Dubs, lost 34 bushels of wheat, 40 bushels of rye, 315 bushels of oats, and 240 bushels of corn. They confiscated barrels of whiskey from other residents, and stole such sundries as accordions, women's bonnets and shawls, buggies and carriages, and even a buffalo robe.

York County Damage Claims, Pennsylvania State Archives, Harrisburg

**

While pausing in New Salem, Captain John Esten Cooke met a pretty Dutch girl, who willingly prepared a bountiful supper for him. "She could not speak English—she could only look amiable, smile, and murmur unintelligible words in an unknown language." She placed milk, coffee, fresh bread, ham, and savory eggs fried with bacon on a small table in a side apartment. Before Cooke could eat, news arrived that General Stuart wanted him to pass somebody through the picket line, and he excused himself. When he returned to his young hostess's house, to his dismay, the feast was gone. A door in the apartment opened onto a street and, tempted by the aroma, a "felonious personage" had entered the house. Every morsel "had vanished down some hungry cavalryman's throat." Despondently, Cooke mounted his horse and trotted ahead to catch up with Stuart's column.

John Esten Cooke, Wearing of the Gray, Being Personal Portraits, Scenes & Adventures of the War. (New York: E.B. Treat & Co., 1867).

**

Near Hanover Junction, Henry Hoff, his wife, and three children peered out their upstairs window as J.E.B. Stuart's lengthy column marched by their farmhouse. Three hours later at dusk when the rear guard passed by, they breathed a sigh of relief. However, an eight-man patrol unexpectedly trotted over to their house, dismounted, and ransacked the first floor and the springhouse. They seized horses and stole clothing, food, and supplies before discovering Hoff's distillery. Delighted, they grabbed several jugs of whiskey, entered a nearby woodlot, and soon were inebriated. Rosanna Hoff was upset that one of the horses was a particular favorite pet. Against her husband's advice, she waited until dark and then dressed in black to avoid detection. She slipped into the woods, found the Rebels sleeping off the whiskey and quietly retrieved her prize horse.

Armand Glatfelter, The Flowering of the North Codorus Palatinate: A History of North Codorus Township. (York, Pennsylvania: Mehl, 1988).

Chapter 2

The Battle of Gettysburg
Wednesday, July 1, 1863

Brigadier General John Buford had deployed two Union cavalry brigades in a vast arc stretching from west of Gettysburg to the northeast, defending likely paths of Confederate attackers. At early dawn, a ripple of gunfire erupted along Carlisle Road north of town. To the west along Chambersburg Pike, Rebels gunned down Cyrus W. James of the 9th New York Cavalry; he is believed to be the first Union soldier to die in the three-day Battle of Gettysburg. The light skirmishing became more ominous when Confederate artillery unlimbered west of Marsh Creek on Lohr's Hill (about four miles west of Gettysburg).

Thirty-one-year-old blacksmith Ephraim Whisler spotted soldiers scurrying about his side yard, and he stormed outside to investigate. Just then, a distant Rebel 12-pound Napoleon gun fired off a solid shot. It struck the turnpike in front of Whisler and plowed up the macadamized crushed stone road bed, showering him with debris. Frightened by the unexpected calamity, he was prostrated by a heart seizure and soon took to his bed. Whisler passed away August 11, among several Adams County residents who would die as an indirect result of the battle. Veterans of the Union cavalry that defended his property later erected a small stone marker commemorating the "first shot" of the Battle of Gettysburg. Whisler's house and yard are now a part of the Gettysburg National Military Park, although seldom visited.

Files of the Library of the Gettysburg National Military Park.
Gettysburg Compiler, 1903.

**

As gunfire crackled in the early morning, thousands of troops from both armies were still heading for Gettysburg. Well to the east in York County, J.E.B. Stuart's travel-weary cavaliers arose in fields surrounding the village of Dover. He had placed armed guards around the town's two hotels so that the cavalrymen could not get drunk. Unknown to them, neither establishment had much alcohol on their premises. A few days before, when the proprietors heard of the Confederate army's approach, all the brandy, whiskey, and other liquor had been hidden in the cellar of the United Brethren Church. Stuart's men never found the stash of "holy water."

George R. Prowell, History of York County, Pennsylvania. (Chicago: J. H. Beers and Co., 1907).

**

Hungry Confederate cavalrymen stopped at one farmhouse near Dover and asked for something to eat. The lady responded that she could prepare some hotcakes. The soldiers sat on a large pile of ashes just outside the back door. When she brought the cakes to them, they asked where all the good Pennsylvania hams they had heard so much about were. She told them ham was hard to come by. What the cavalrymen didn't know was that the ash pile on which they were sitting concealed the family's supply of hams.

Ronald L. Botterbusch, Civil War Hours in Dover Township – When Confederates Passed Through, A History of Dover Township, York County, Pennsylvania: 1790s–1990s. (Dover, Pa.: Dover Township Board of Supervisors, 1994).

**

The Hampton Battery, a Union reserve artillery battery from Pittsburgh, passed through Taneytown, Maryland, as the big guns rolled towards Gettysburg. The crewmen camped the night of June 30 on the Alexander McAllister farm a mile west of Taneytown, pitching tents in the back yard. As they departed on July 1 for the battlefield, they were forced to say goodbye to their concerts from the seven-member string band. The music had helped the soldiers temporarily forget about the sadness over recent losses and struggles. Their organizer, namesake, and captain, Robert B. Hampton, had been killed at the recent Battle of Chancellorsville.

However, the bandsmen could not properly care for the instruments while preparing to march into battle. The guitars, violins, and a bass viol were unloaded from a supply wagon and left in the care of the McAllister family. They stored the musical instruments for several months and eventually shipped them back to Pittsburgh. One well used guitar had already been returned to one of the musicians, who had been wounded during the fighting at Gettysburg and was recuperating in a Baltimore hospital. To the injured man's delight, two of McAllister's fair daughters paid him a visit to personally deliver the guitar. Grateful battery members stayed in touch with the Maryland family after the war.

William Clark, History of Hampton Battery F Independent Pennsylvania Light Artillery. (Akron and Pittsburgh: The Werner Company, 1909).

**

Despite the presence of Buford's cavalry brigades, most Gettysburg residents went on with their daily lives. Nathaniel Lightner and his neighbor, John Taney, planned to mow a meadow behind the orchard on Lightner's Baltimore Pike farm. The morning was hot and sultry, and they apparently could not hear the noise from the growing combat. After mowing for some time, Taney turned to Lightner and suggested, "I could do better if I had a little whiskey to drink." Lightner, wanting Taney to keep working, replied, "I can soon get you some." Grabbing an empty jug, he set off for town to fetch the booze. He entered town about 9:00 a.m., where he could see a long line of smoke rising from along the Chambersburg Pike to the west. Lightner and a friend watched the arrival of Major General Oliver O. Howard's Eleventh Corps, and then they headed over to Seminary Ridge to see the action. They high-tailed it back into town when Confederate artillery started firing in earnest.

Tim Smith, Adams County Historical Society.

**

As the 76th New York approached the battlefield, the column halted on a hill that offered a commanding view of Gettysburg. Near a farmhouse on the crest, Major General John F. Reynolds of the First Army Corps and other generals and officers surveyed the distant battle through their field glasses as couriers and scouts scurried in with reports. A stream of refugees rushed by, heading for safety and clutching what valuables they could carry.

The hungry soldiers of the 76th looked longingly across the road at a long line of cherry trees, their branches drooping under the weight of a bumper crop of ripe fruit. Major Andrew Grover rode down from the group of officers on the crest and addressed his men, "Boys, the General (brigade commander Lysander Cutler) charges you to be very particular to keep strictly within the rules, and not meddle with those cherry *trees*!" He emphasized the word "trees" for effect, and added, "Be sure you don't break the *trees* down!" Grover turned his horse up the road and stared at the knot of officers, his back turned to the regiment. His infantrymen picked up on the hint and realized its hidden message—the trees themselves were off limits from harm, but the cherries were indeed fair game. Soon, the trees were stripped bare while the commanders deliberately looked the other way. It turned out that the farmer, by his manner and conversation, had convinced the generals that he was an ardent secessionist, and they had decided to teach him a lesson. Grover's men were the beneficiaries of this thievery.

During the subsequent battle of Gettysburg, the farmhouse was riddled with bullets and shell fragments, and the farmer faced financial ruin. Lieutenant Abram Smith opined, "Not one in the Union army, who understood his political status, mourned over his loss." They did mourn Grover's loss, as the major was instantly killed by a Minié ball later that morning during the early stages of the 76th's deployment.

Abram P. Smith, History of the Seventy-sixth Regiment, New York Volunteers. (Cortland, New York: Truair, Smith and Miles, printers, 1867)

**

The Iron Brigade was a celebrated Union infantry unit comprised of veteran regiments from the "west" (Wisconsin, Michigan, and Indiana). As the black-hatted soldiers advanced through open woods and down a gentle slope towards Willoughby Run, they pushed Brigadier General James J. Archer's Confederates ahead of them. One 2nd Wisconsin soldier seized Archer, making the Maryland native the first of Lee's generals to be captured during the war. Guards escorted him and scores of sullen prisoners to the rear. Union Major General Abner Doubleday, a pre-war army acquaintance, offered his hand and good-naturedly exclaimed, "Good morning, Archer! How are you? I am glad to see you!" Archer angrily retorted, "Well, I am *not* glad to see *you,* by a ____ sight, Doubleday!" General Archer would spend months in the Johnson's Island prison camp in northern Ohio before being exchanged.

In an open field on the front lines, the Wisconsin boys were still celebrating their success when a gunshot rang out from a Confederate hidden in a distant woodlot. Sergeant Jonathan Bryan was waving his hat and cheering the apparent victory, when the Minié ball struck home. He slumped to the ground, his lifeblood draining away. A Pennsylvania native, Bryan had moved to Wisconsin before the war, and he never could have dreamed then that his army service would eventually bring him back to die in the dirt of the Keystone State.

Robert K. Beecham, Gettysburg: The Pivotal Battle of the Civil War. (Chicago: A.C. McClurg, 1911).

**

During times of crisis and personal stress, men react in divergent ways. Some rely on faith, finding comfort in the words of the Lord. Others gain courage to face what may come from friends and companions, seeking mutual strength. A few panic and cannot make decisions. Still others find solace in the bottle or, as one Union soldier termed it, "Master Whiskey." Private Daniel Appleby, a 22-year-old infantryman from Shade Gap in central Pennsylvania, years before suffered through the loss of his father, killed by an angry horse's wicked kick. As the oldest son, Daniel inherited the task of managing the family farm. When his brothers were old enough to assume the task, Appleby enlisted in the 149th Pennsylvania in August 1862. So far, he had not seen any significant combat, nor had most officers in the regiment.

The "Bucktails," nicknamed for their penchant of wearing the tails of Whitetail Deer on their hats, were in Colonel Roy Stone's brigade. As they prepared for battle, Appleby watched several commissioned officers become inebriated, even though it was still morning. The regiment went into action shortly after 11:30 a.m., and Stone was soon wounded and incapacitated. Junior officers issued ill-advised orders to advance into an exposed position in a clearing near the railroad cut. There, they were decimated, and the survivors hugged the ground. Appleby complained, "...The enemy advanced on us and we were compelled to crawl out and fall back to our former position on the pike, with heavy loss, all owing to our drunken leaders." Only seven of the fifty-four men in his Company I emerged unscathed by the end of the long afternoon.

After surviving the carnage of war, Dan Appleby mustered out in 1865 and went home, returning to the farm. He later worked for the railroad for over twenty years. On Feb. 5, 1903, almost forty years after Gettysburg, he was struck and killed by an engine at a freight station.

Dairy of Daniel C. M. Appleby, quoted by Milan Simonich, Gettysburg: Profiles in Courage / Daniel Appleby, Pittsburgh Post-Gazette, July 6, 2003.

**

The elderly Gettysburg citizen, John Burns, is often reported to be the only civilian to take up arms to fight with the Union Army at Gettysburg. Such an assertion is not true, however. The 12th Massachusetts had its own "John Burns" in its ranks as it fought along the Mummasburg Road north of Gettysburg. A slender boy the soldiers estimated to be sixteen had tagged along when the regiment marched through Emmitsburg, becoming enmeshed with Company A. He went into battle on Oak Ridge on July 1 and was wounded in the arm and thigh by Confederate fire. The boyish volunteer was carried beyond the crest of the ridge and given water. He was later taken away to a field hospital, and his comrades never heard from him again. Lieutenant Colonel Benjamin Cook recalled, "His very name is unknown; for he was never mustered into service." Cook may have never known the civilian's name, but J. W. Weakley survived his wounds. One of eight children of an eccentric indigent mountaineer, the illiterate Weakley later enlisted in the 13th Pennsylvania Cavalry. In November 1864, the unsung Gettysburg hero drowned ignominiously when he suffered an epileptic seizure and fell into in a camp cesspool.

Benjamin F. Cook, History of the Twelfth Massachusetts Volunteers. (Boston: Twelfth (Webster) Regiment Association, 1882).
George Kimball, A Young Hero of Gettysburg, Century Magazine, November 1886.

**

Old Burns and young Weakley were not the only Pennsylvania civilians to join in fighting the invaders. At times, armed "bushwhackers" fired from various hiding places along the path of Lee's army. Luckily, they rarely hit anyone, and they nearly always dodged patrols sent in pursuit as they fled from the scene. Colonel Clement Evans of the 31st Georgia wrote home that these random bushwhackers were a good thing, as they kept the soldiers from straggling too far from the column. However, in at least one case, the cat-and-mouse game became deadly. In a forested mountain pass just west of the Adams County village of Cashtown, Henry Hahn and some friends ambushed and picked off a mounted Rebel, who later died from his wounds. Vitriolic Confederate General Jubal Early threatened

38

to burn down the entire village unless the cowardly perpetrators were located. They were not found, but the buildings were spared the torch when cooler heads prevailed.

Other citizens, too honorable to be ambushers but still wanting a shot at the Rebels, marched along with Union infantry regiments. During the June 26, 1863, skirmishing north of Gettysburg on the Henry Witmer farm, an unnamed Gettysburg resident took up arms and fought alongside the 26th Pennsylvania Volunteer Militia, an emergency infantry regiment that contained a company of men from the local Pennsylvania College. The identity of this civilian hero has also been lost, but perhaps he was a fellow student, friend, or family member of the enlisted soldiers.

At the Skirmish of Wrightsville on June 28, an entire company of armed black volunteers from the surrounding area defended a portion of the earthworks protecting the town and its vital railroad bridge. They were not mustered into Federal service, and all of them wore civilian clothing. One unfortunate man was decapitated by a Rebel artillery shell. His identity remains unknown. In addition to these blacks, a handful of civilians from York also shouldered muskets and fought in the entrenchments alongside the soldiers, whereas three full companies of volunteers from Columbia, their courage perhaps lacking, hastily retreated before the Rebels approached.

H. M. M. Richards, Pennsylvania's Emergency Men at Gettysburg. (Reading, Pennsylvania: self-published, 1895).
Files of the York County Heritage Trust.

**

During the noontime lull in the fighting west of Gettysburg, Union soldiers regrouped, paused to replenish ammunition, and rested as much as possible. Stewards and other noncombatants helped remove some of the wounded to the rear, but the task was daunting and the workers too few. Soldiers still capable of fighting were ordered to stay in line and not assist the taxed medical crews. Hundreds of unfortunate men lay where they fell, and others could be seen slowly crawling or limping from the field. Robert Beecham of the 2nd Wisconsin noted one badly wounded man from his company using a pair of muskets picked up on the field as crutches. The last Beecham saw of the injured man, he was working his way painfully up a slope towards an aid station in the rear. The wound necessitated the amputation of his leg, but he lived for many years after the war.

Robert K. Beecham, Gettysburg: The Pivotal Battle of the Civil War. (Chicago: A.C. McClurg, 1911).

**

Part of the Iron Brigade defended an open woodlot on McPherson's Ridge. Their attention was drawn to a Rebel colonel, who sat calmly astride a large mule in back of his advancing battle line. He kept calling out, "Give them ___, boys!" and urged his men

39

forward. A Yankee bullet knocked his cap from his head. Without missing a beat, the colonel reached out and snatched his hat before it fell to the ground. Placing it back on his head, he continued exhorting his men. He and his braying mule were soon lost from sight in the gunsmoke.

The Iron Brigade was shattered that afternoon, along with their attackers. The ferocity of the close order combat they experienced at Gettysburg is illustrated perhaps best by the color guard of the 24th Michigan, the veteran brigade's newest regiment. During the fighting, fourteen different men held the flag aloft. Eleven were wounded, nine fatally. The proud old flag, begrimed and in tatters, was later replaced by several leading citizens of Detroit.

Orson B. Curtis, History of the Twenty-fourth Michigan of the Iron Brigade. (Detroit: Winn & Hammond, 1891).

**

The fighting spread north of Gettysburg, where elements of both the First and Eleventh Corps faced Richard Ewell's oncoming Confederates. Captain William Waldron of the 16th Maine tried to steady his company, shouting that they should keep their cool and aim low. He knew that jittery soldiers often fired too high, completely missing their intended targets. While his men crouched behind a low stone wall that offered some cover and psychological comfort, he stood and peered westward into the fields of John Forney's farm, teeming with a long line of Rebels. A Minié ball sliced into his neck, narrowing missing his jugular vein. He refused to head to the rear for treatment. Instead, Waldron steadied himself by grabbing hold of a tree with one hand. He used the other to try to staunch the flow of blood. He lived.

Bradley L. Gottfried, Brigades of Gettysburg. (Cambridge, Massachusetts: Da Capo Press, 2002).

**

As fighting intensified in mid-afternoon, Rebels threatened to overwhelm Colonel Roy Stone's untried Union brigade in its isolated position astride the McPherson farm. To encourage his 150th Pennsylvania, Lieutenant Colonel Henry S. Huidekoper ordered the standard bearer, Sergeant Samuel Peiffer, to move forward with the colors. Peiffer, "a large man with boundless courage," responded without hesitating and walked ahead steadily despite galling enemy fire. The regiment, drawing strength from his bold action, pushed ahead and halted the Confederates. Not long after 3 p.m., the Rebels renewed their attack, and their fire toppled several men of the color guard. Peiffer defiantly waved his flag at the oncoming enemy before he too fell with a mortal wound.

Pennsylvania at Gettysburg: Ceremonies at the dedication of the monuments erected by the commonwealth of Pennsylvania... (Pennsylvania Battlefield Commission, 1913).

Not far away, the color sergeant of the 143rd Pennsylvania, Ben Crippen, also turned towards the oncoming enemy as his regiment retired. He raised his fist and angrily shook it at the Rebels. Moments later, he was gunned down and left to bleed to death. His valor was widely admired by onlookers, including Lieutenant General A.P. Hill, commander of the Confederates who opposed the badly outnumbered Pennsylvanians. Years later, the regiment's participation in the battle was memorialized by a marble monument, which depicts Crippen shaking his fist at oncoming Rebels.

Files of the Library of Gettysburg National Military Park

**

Both the First and Eleventh Corps began to withdraw towards Gettysburg. Some men ran away, while others turned around and fought to the death. As Rebels swarmed around the guns of Battery B, 4th U.S. Artillery, a crewman faced a group of Rebels who threatened his artillery piece. With a mighty swing of his swab rod, he broke the neck of the enemy squad leader. However, the remaining Southerners killed the valiant gunner with a series of vicious bayonet thrusts.

In contrast, stories abound of men who whimpered in the face of danger and slunk away to hide. As the 76th New York marched by a stone wall near the railroad, Captain Herschel Pierce of Company A spotted a soldier "nicely rolled up in a blanket," lying behind the wall with his head covered up. Considering the care with which the soldier was covered to be unusual for a dead man, Pierce decided to investigate. The man proved to be very much alive.

"What are you doing here?" thundered Pierce. "Get up!"

"I can't. I am awfully wounded," came the forlorn response from under the blanket.

"Where?" inquired the captain.

"Here," said the man, pointing to his side.

Pierce could find no blood or wound. The man explained he must have been mistaken and pointed to a different place on his body, but Pierce again saw no injury. Several times he changed the location of the alleged wound until a frustrated Pierce shouted, "Get up, you coward! Fall in!" Even though the shirker was not a member of his regiment, Pierce kept him in the forefront of the thickest fighting the rest of the day.

Abram P. Smith, History of the Seventy-sixth Regiment, New York Volunteers. (Cortland, New York: Truair, Smith and Miles, printers, 1867)

**

As the 150th Pennsylvania retreated, Captain George W. Jones was able to keep his company in column, with fewer Rebels threatening his route than other companies farther to the north. He had entered the western outskirts of Gettysburg without incident when his men ran into a Confederate regiment coming down an intersecting street. A field officer, riding at its head, ordered the Yankees to halt. Before Jones could reply, Private Terrence O'Connor coolly remarked, "We take no orders from the likes of you!" He raised his musket, took careful aim, and dropped the officer to the ground.

Thomas Chamberlin, History of the One hundred and fiftieth regiment, Pennsylvania Volunteers, Second Regiment, Bucktail Brigade. (Philadelphia: F. McManus, Jr., 1905).

**

The Confederates, sensing an apparent victory when they saw the Yankees withdrawing, pressed forward in pursuit. A few noncombatants in the rear lines stopped to refresh themselves from abandoned houses on the outskirts of Gettysburg. Spencer Welch was the regimental surgeon of the 13th South Carolina in Perrin's Brigade. After watching the brigade drive off a line of Union defenders, he and some colleagues entered a house, "from which everyone had fled except an extremely old man. A churn of excellent buttermilk had been left, and I with some other doctors helped ourselves. Someone near by shot at us as we came out and barely missed us." A shaken, but grateful Dr. Welch returned to the field hospital to tend to the wounded throughout the night, not getting any rest until after daylight on July 2.

Spencer Glasgow Welch, A Confederate Surgeon's Letters to His Wife. (New York and Washington: The Neale Publishing Company, 1911).

**

Thousands of soldiers wounded in the terrible fighting at Gettysburg faced days, weeks, months, and even years of recuperation and rehabilitation. The story of nineteen-year-old J. Robinson Balsley illustrates the plight of many of these men. The twelfth of fifteen children of a couple in rural Connellsville, Pennsylvania, he worked as a carpenter with his father until the outbreak of the Civil War, when he enlisted as a private in the 142nd Pennsylvania and served in Virginia. Now, he was back in his native Pennsylvania, fighting on Edward McPherson's tenant farm west of Gettysburg. He was desperately wounded in both thighs and fell about two hundred yards from where his corps commander, Major General John F. Reynolds, was killed. As young Balsley lay crippled and bleeding, three successive waves of Confederate attackers passed over him. He lay there for three long days until the Rebels had departed.

Barely alive when found by Union searchers, he was taken to a hospital improvised at the Catholic Church in Gettysburg. He lay there, hovering between life and death, until July 17, when he had regained enough strength to be taken to the Cotton Factory Hospital in

Harrisburg. Youth and a hardy constitution triumphed and, in the latter part of December, he was shipped by train to the Cliffburn Barracks in Washington, although utterly unfit for the hardships of camp. Reassigned to Company A of the 7th Veteran Reserves, Balsley was called again to the front lines when J.E.B. Stuart's cavalry threatened Washington during its daring 1864 raid. Despite his infirmity, he continued in military service until January 25, 1865, when he was finally discharged. He returned home to the carpenter's trade and later established a prosperous lumberyard.

John W. Jordan, Genealogical and Personal History of Fayette County. (Lewis Historical Publishing Co., 1912).

**

By mid-1863, it was unusual to see women still accompanying regiments to the battlefield. One exception was Elmina Spencer, the matron of the 147th New York. The 43-year-old former Oswego school teacher rode a heavily laden horse, packing her bedding, extra clothes, and 350 pounds of supplies for the sick and wounded on its back. Included were two knapsacks and two haversacks with materials to make tea, coffee, and beef broth to nourish her patients. Her husband, a medical steward, had not accompanied her to Gettysburg, having stayed in Maryland to tend to a teamster badly burned when an ammunition wagon accidentally exploded.

As the battle raged on July 1, Elmina entered a barnyard near Gettysburg and began brewing coffee in iron kettles over campfires, passing out steaming cups to wounded soldiers from the Eleventh Corps. She ignored orders to head to the rear after news arrived that the 147th had nearly been destroyed, and instead pressed forward to front-line aid stations to minister to the wounded. Later, she built campfires on Cemetery Hill and passed out hot refreshments to retreating Union soldiers as they reassembled there.

Life after the war was harsh. Her husband's health had been broken by the war, and he was unable to work. The couple moved to Kansas in 1873, but two years later, Robert Spencer died. Elmina's sufferings were only beginning. In short order, she also lost her parents and her mother-in-law, and her house burned down in a prairie wildfire. The widow returned to Oswego and lived on a military pension, dying in 1912. Mrs. Spencer was truly one of the unsung heroines of Gettysburg.

Seventeenth Publication of the Oswego County Historical Society. (Oswego, New York: Palladium Times, Inc., 1954).

**

North of Gettysburg, part of the Union Eleventh Corps was in danger of being overwhelmed by advancing Confederates, who were supported with several batteries of artillery. On a knoll on the Blocher farm just west of the Harrisburg Pike stood Battery G,

4th U.S. Artillery, commanded by a 19-year-old lieutenant from Buffalo, New York, named Bayard Wilkeson. A fragment of a bursting Confederate shell struck the young artilleryman in the leg. He quickly made a tourniquet to staunch the flow of blood and calmly cut off the mangled leg with a pocket knife. He was carried behind the lines to the county poorhouse, where he was suffering greatly from shock and loss of blood. The gallant teenager asked for some water, and someone handed him a canteen. Before he could take a sip, a wounded soldier lying next to him begged "for God's sake give me some." The stricken officer passed the canteen to the desperate man, who drained every drop. Wilkeson smiled, turned slightly, and died.

Final Report on the Battlefield of Gettysburg (New York at Gettysburg). New York Monuments Commission for the Battlefields of Gettysburg and Chattanooga. (Albany, NY: J. B. Lyon Company, 1902).

**

Several soldiers from the 154th New York were captured as the regiment retreated from the fields just northeast of Gettysburg under pressure from two of Jubal Early's brigades. Newell Burch noted an act of kindness from one of his captors, "The first impression I had of Southern hospitality I received was a basket of cherries from a Reb, as I was being escorted to the rear by a Reb on each side. He said, 'Here, Yank, you will need these before I shall.'" Burch later termed this the last act of kindness he received from the Confederates, because he spent the next two years in a prison camp.

Newell Burch diary, Minnesota Historical Society; quoted by Mark Dunkelman and Michael J. Winey, The Hardtack Regiment in the Brickyard Fight, The Gettysburg Magazine, #8, January 1993.

**

Earlier in the day, fifteen-year-old Albertus McCreary and some friends had walked towards Seminary Ridge to see the action, but returned to town when artillery shells began falling near them. When retreating Union soldiers jammed the streets in the late afternoon, McCreary and his family set out tin dippers and buckets of water, an act of kindness greatly appreciated by the tired combatants. A small drummer boy ran up to the steps of the McCreary house (at the corner of Baltimore and High streets), handed his drum to Albertus, and told him, "Keep this for me." Albertus took it downstairs into the cellar and hid it under a pile of wood shavings. The drum had the boy's name and regiment printed on it in red letters. However, young McCreary never saw the drummer again and received no reply to a letter sent to him. He presumed the drummer boy had been killed in the fighting.

Albertus McCreary, Gettysburg: A Boy's Experience of the Battle. Manuscript in the Library of the Gettysburg National Military Park.

After the Union forces retreated through Gettysburg, a little girl named Laura Bergstresser stood at the second-story window of her parents' house on Baltimore Street. Her brother, sick with typhoid fever, lay in a nearby room. Laura, daughter of the local Methodist minister, peered through a bowed shutter at the confusion below in the street. Suddenly, an artillery shell struck the outside wall just beside the wooden shutter, tearing out a large hole and scattering pieces of brick, mortar, and plaster all around the room. Luckily, the shell did not explode but instead rebounded and fell into the street. Laura was so terrified by the near-miss that she raced downstairs, bounded across the street, and ran into her neighbors' house for safety. Federal soldiers hiding in the Pierce house informed Laura that it was a stray shot and might never happen again. Reassured that she was just as safe in her own home, Laura ran back to her parents.

Matilda "Tillie" Pierce Alleman, At Gettysburg, or, What a Girl Saw and Heard of the Battle. A True Narrative. (New York: W. Lake Borland, 1889).

The regimental surgeons of the 147th New York and 14th Brooklyn established a temporary hospital in a large hotel on the south side of Gettysburg. During the late morning, wounded men streamed back from the battlefield west of town and soon filled the hospital to capacity. Many were desperately wounded, but several shirkers had used minor wounds as an excuse to head for the rear. They roamed the hotel and ransacked it, guzzling its supply of liquor and getting intoxicated.

In the afternoon, about a dozen of these men peered out the windows at the street, which was clogged with retreating soldiers from the Eleventh Corps. Soon, pursuing Rebels came into sight. The Brooklyn boys opened fire from the hospital's windows, drawing a return volley that peppered the building but did no major harm. They scrambled out of the hotel and lined up in front, as if to protect the hospital against the entire Confederate army. Their drunken bravado was short-lived however, as a Rebel squadron leveled their rifles and took aim.

Luckily, one of the surgeons was returning to the hotel after visiting wounded officers of his regiment who were being housed in another part of town. He ordered the Confederates not to shoot the wounded men. A Rebel officer complied, but he turned to the surgeon and demanded, "Disarm them, then, or I will have every man of them shot." The doctor ordered his patients to give up their arms and go back inside the hospital. All quickly obeyed, except for three or four hotheads who declared they would never surrender. Some Confederates opened fire, shooting one Union soldier through the heart. He sprawled across the hotel's steps, which were soon covered in blood. The brave surgeon managed to save the lives of the other men, once or twice pushing aside the barrels of enemy rifles as they were about to fire.

Finally, with assistance from other onlookers, he wrenched the muskets from the hands of his remaining malcontents, who surrendered.

When matters finally quieted, the surgeon's attention was drawn across the street to a "considerably intoxicated" mounted Confederate officer, who brandished a pistol and declared that he would sack and burn the hospital because the wounded men had fired from its windows. The Rebel rode over to the surgeon and bragged, "I say, doctor, don't we Louisianans fight like h--l?" He held up several trophies he had obviously picked up from the battlefield, although he boasted he had personally captured them from Yankee officers through his fighting prowess. The surgeon, mindful that his wounded men had indeed violated the accepted rules of civilized warfare by firing from a marked hospital, flattered the Rebel about his martial skills. Satisfied, the drunken officer rode off proudly, forgetting about his plans to torch the building. As the afternoon wore on, the now disarmed and more sober New Yorkers sat in the curbstone side-by-side with their Louisiana captors. Men who a short time before were ready to defend the hospital with their lives now calmly chatted with their enemy who had been equally anxious to shoot them down.

Criswell Johnson, History of Oswego County, NY, With Illustrations and Biographical Sketches of Some of its Prominent Men and Pioneers. (Philadelphia: L. H. Everts & Co., 1877).

**

The rallying point for the retreating Union troops was Cemetery Hill. On its summit, the impressive Evergreen Cemetery gatehouse served as a landmark. Caretaker Elizabeth Thorn and her mother-in-law spent the day baking bread, slicing it with a butcher knife and passing it out to soldiers as fast as she could. She placed tubs of water outside the building for the thirsty men. Six months pregnant at the time, she later wrote, "All the time our little boys were pumping and carrying water to fill the tubs. They handed water to the soldiers and worked and helped this way until their poor little hands were blistered…"

The Gettysburg Times Centennial Edition, June 28, 1963.

**

The scattered Federals reorganized on Cemetery Hill and, as evening approached without any additional Rebel attacks, cooks began preparing dinner for the famished soldiers. Confederate artillery unexpectedly opened a brisk fire from the west, and the first shell exploded directly under a kettle in which a servant was boiling food for some officers. The servant was untouched by the shell fragments, but his pack horse, an "old shave-tail," was torn to pieces. The cook was so badly frightened that he stood like a statue for several moments, as if paralyzed. He was "as white as a corpse." Captain Eminel Halstead, General Doubleday's assistant adjutant general, later wrote, "It was the most laughable sight I ever saw in battle. We dined and supped on hardtack that night as our provisions went up with the kettle."

Halstead, E. P., The First Day of the Battle of Gettysburg, A paper read before the District of Columbia Commandery of the Military Order of the Loyal Legion of the United States, March 2, 1887. Volume 1, Papers 1-26, March-April 1897.

**

Throughout the long day, tens of thousands of soldiers from both armies were still approaching Gettysburg. Among these reinforcements was the Union Twelfth Corps, which marched from Littlestown, Pennsylvania, towards Gettysburg as the boom of artillery resonated. In an effort to hasten them forward and, with roads jammed with troops, officers at times led their men on cross-country journeys. The 123rd New York left the road and pushed ahead as fast as possible through woods, over hills and fences, and across rain-soaked fields and swampy terrain, "until the boys were completely exhausted." They arrived near Gettysburg in the late afternoon and, by nightfall, took position on Wolf Hill as a reserve. Arrayed in a battle line, they slept with their guns by their sides.

Henry C. Morhous, Reminiscences of the 123d Regiment, N.Y.S.V. (Greenwich, New York: People's Journal Book and Job Office, 1879).

**

Meanwhile, J.E.B. Stuart now hoped to connect with Ewell's Corps at Carlisle. His cavalry and supply wagons kicked up a towering cloud of dust visible for miles as they rode northwesterly through rural York County. Along the way, they raided farms and villages for food, provisions and, most importantly, fresh horses to replace their jaded mounts.

After riding for miles on the hot, dry late afternoon, Stuart halted his column in Dillsburg for rest and water. Some soldiers robbed the local post office, figuring it was official U.S. government property and, as such, was liable to confiscation during wartime. They snatched up all the money they could find and pocketed stamps and other valuables. One even took the coat of postmaster A. N. Eslinger. Stuart cut short his cavaliers' merriment and hustled them on towards Carlisle, where they arrived at dark to find Union militia there instead of Ewell.

A. N. Eslinger, Local History of Dillsburg, Pa. (Dillsburg, Pennsylvania.: Dillsburg Bulletin Printing, 1902).

**

Stuart unlimbered artillery on hills overlooking Carlisle. After lobbing a few shells at militia defenders, Stuart torched the town's gasworks and the nearby U.S. Army barracks.

One of his brigadier generals, Fitzhugh Lee, had been stationed there before the Civil War. Near the barracks lived Luther A. Line, a 27-year-old nurseryman and amateur historian who collected photographs of officers serving at the barracks. Line was home that e resting from the excitement of Ewell's Corps' two-day visit to Carlisle.

Line was surprised when a Rebel sergeant entered his parlor. It proved to be his friends from before the war, a former Dickinson College student named Samuel W who mentioned, "General Lee is outside and wants to see you." Line walked outside an an unfamiliar officer who said he was General Lee. Line replied that he knew a Lieut Lee who some years before had been stationed at the Carlisle Barracks. "Well," answere Confederate, "I am he." They reminisced a short while before Lee excused himself to r his troops. Line returned to his parlor and noted that his photograph of young Fitzhugh was missing. He surmised that Sergeant Weller had recognized his commander's picture pocketed it as a souvenir. Weller, a member of Lee's signal corps, was reported miss following the Battle of Gettysburg and never heard from again.

Years after the war, Fitz Lee visited the Carlisle Indian School. Luther Line used occasion to renew his acquaintance with the former general. Line mentioned the loss of Lee's photograph years ago during his last visit to town. Lee expressed regret at the theft and promised to send another picture when he returned home. Line eagerly watched the mail, but no photo ever came. General Lee probably forgot about his promise.

Biographical Annals of Cumberland County, Pennsylvania. (Chicago: The Genealogical Publishing Co., 1905).

**

Many Civil War soldiers were superstitious, prone to premonitions of death and portents of victory or defeat. The 2nd Pennsylvania Reserves, en route to Gettysburg on July 1, wearily lay down in a "fine open woods" in the late afternoon. Happy to be back on their native soil, the men lolled around and listened to the strains of regimental bands wafting in the twilight air. On a beautiful and warm early summer evening, the men were refreshed by an abundance of rations, although, ominously, they each received sixty rounds of ammunition. Evan Woodward and his comrades settled in, knowing that tomorrow they would likely be in battle. He later wrote, "While lying here, through the branches above, amidst the bright sunshine, a large star was discerned shining over us with all the brilliancy of a heavenly visitant, which was gazed upon by all with great interest, and received as an omen of victory, which, happily, it proved to be." However, for some of Woodward's companions, the star would signal their last night on Earth.

Evan M. Woodward, Our Campaigns…, (Philadelphia: John E. Potter, 1865).

Chapter 3

The Battle of Gettysburg
Thursday, July 2, 1863

Gettysburg residents awoke to find their borough firmly in Confederate hands, with Union defenders stretched for two miles south of town in defensive lines resembling a giant fishhook. The apex was Cemetery Hill, with the barb on nearby Culp's Hill. The shaft was along Cemetery Ridge, a low crest that ran southward to two small mountains, the Round Tops. Other Federal defenders occupied supporting positions to the rear. Lee's army roughly paralleled this fishhook in a wider arc. Throughout the morning and early afternoon, there was little hard combat between the armies, but sharpshooters and skirmishers claimed a number of lives.

George Nixon III was a forty-two-year-old private in Company B of the 73rd Ohio. A native of Washington, Pennsylvania, Nixon married his sweetheart Margaret Trimmer in 1843. He later moved to scenic Ross County in south-central Ohio, where he bought a farm and raised nine children. Despite his brood, he responded to a recruiting call and enrolled in the Union army at nearby Waverly on November 9, 1861. Skirmishing in the open fields west of Cemetery Ridge, Nixon was struck by Confederate bullets in his right hip and side. He was left lying in the sunshine throughout the day, as the enemy fire was too hot for his comrades to come to his assistance. The stricken soldier cried out in pain for help and water, but no one dared reach him.

Finally, after darkness had brought an end to most of the shooting, twenty-year-old Private Richard Enderlin, one of Company B's musicians, responded to the forlorn cries. Waiting until clouds blocked the bright moonlight, the German immigrant crawled across the field and located the wounded man. Over the next couple of hours, he dragged Nixon slowly back towards the safety of the Federal lines. When he thought he was close enough, Enderlin stood up with Nixon in tow and dashed back to his admiring comrades.

For his bravery, young Enderlin was immediately promoted to sergeant and, years later, received the Medal of Honor for his courageous and compassionate action. However, his heroism came too late for Nixon. Two days after being wounded, he breathed his last and died in an Eleventh Corps' field hospital. He was buried nearby, but his body was later exhumed and reinterred in the new National Cemetery. In November, Abraham Lincoln dedicated the 3,500 graves with "a few appropriate remarks." The dead Buckeye, lying not far from the wooden platform where Lincoln spoke, was the great-grandfather of the 37th

President of the United States, Richard M. Nixon...

paid a visit to his...

...windows...

...despite the danger, one fearless (and ...cherry tree in the backyard of the McCreary house, on the southern ...Gettysburg. He calmly began to pick cherries, ignoring the whistling bullets. Another Confederate, hearing that the family's pet rabbits were hungry, volunteered to dash outside and feed them. He managed to accomplish the task without getting shot.

Albertus McCreary, Gettysburg: A Boy's Experience of the Battle. Manuscript in the Library of the Gettysburg National Military Park.

**

Skirmishing along the Emmitsburg Road south of Gettysburg, men from Lieutenant Thomas Thornburg's company of the 8th Ohio shot down a Rebel who had "four fair sized hams strung on his shoulders, and another with a cheese as big as a grindstone." The foragers never got to enjoy their booty.

Martin Graham, A Gallant Defense, Civil War Times Illustrated, Volume XXV, Number 3.

**

At one point in the skirmishing with the 8th Ohio, one Southerner screamed out, "Don't fire, Yanks!" Obliging the persuasive cry, firing ceased among those within earshot. Soon, a Confederate soldier warily emerged from his hiding place behind a large tree not thirty yards from the Union position. With his rifle slung over his shoulder, the Rebel calmly walked out into an intervening wheatfield and knelt beside a wounded Yankee lying amid the crushed wheat stalks. After giving him water, the Confederate scurried among the wounded from both armies, parsing out the rest of his canteen's contents without regard for the color of the wounded men's uniforms. The stunned Buckeyes held their fire and admiringly sent up a loud cheer, "Bully for you, Johnny! Bully!" When the last of the water was gone, the

Reb stood up and hiked back to his sheltering tree. There, he ducked down, unslung his musket, and called out, "Down Yanks, we're going to fire." The shooting soon resumed. The identity of this brave hero remains unknown.

John Michael Priest, Into the Fight: Pickett's Charge at Gettysburg. (Shippensburg, Pennsylvania: 1998).

**

Still riding towards Gettysburg on the morning of July 2, one of J.E.B. Stuart's brigades, commanded by wealthy South Carolina planter Wade Hampton III, passed through the Cumberland County village of Clear Springs. Residents had taken horses to remote woods and hidden the valuables from their post office in a haymow to prevent thievery. In the midst of the village stood a nondescript general store owned by a merchant named John Dick. Several Rebels helped themselves to Dick's inventory of new shoes, casually tossing their worn out castoffs into a heap on the front porch before riding off towards Gettysburg.

Victor Neubaum, Dillsburg Community News, September 14, 1988, based upon accounts from the Northern York County Historical Society.

**

A patrol from Company B of the 3rd Virginia Cavalry rode up to a Cumberland County farmhouse and dismounted. Knocks on the door were answered by a mother holding a baby, and the Rebels asked if they could purchase some food, as they had not eaten much for days. She snapped, "I have nothing and if I did, I'd not give it to you." As one soldier stepped closer, she proclaimed, "You dirty Rebels will get nothing from me. I'd like to see the whole lot of you die!" One suddenly snatched the baby from her arms and insinuated he would eat it if she did not produce some other food. She screamed in terror, her bravado gone. The man offered to trade the baby for food. The shaken woman complied, entering her house and dishing out bacon, ham, fowl, and bread and butter to the famished soldiers. One later wrote, "We had a glorious feast and took the remainder back to camp after paying her for all we had taken." The Confederate money was worthless, but the woman believed she had saved her baby's life.

Fitzhugh Lee letter to J.T. Zug, August 15, 1882, Cumberland County Historical Society, Carlisle, Pennsylvania.

**

After belatedly arriving in Adams County, Stuart's Confederate cavalry ran into Union troopers northeast of Gettysburg near the village of Hunterstown. Days earlier, the diligent pastor of the Great Conewago Presbyterian Church and the nearby Lower Marsh Creek Church, the Reverend John R. Warner, had gathered all of his past sermons, his notes, both church's vital records, and other valuable papers and sent them off to Chambersburg for safekeeping. He was concerned that the Rebels might visit his town and perhaps destroy the church or the papers. He was correct in assuming the Rebels would visit Hunterstown and, after the battle, both of his churches became field hospitals. Luckily for Warner, his papers were not disturbed during their storage in Confederate-occupied Chambersburg. However, for some reason, the preacher did not reclaim the documents when the Rebels retired to Virginia. The papers were all lost on July 30, 1864, when John McCausland's Confederate cavalry brigade burned much of the Chambersburg.

ᶜCumberland and Adams Counties. (Chicago: Warner, Beers & Co., 1886).

**

After the combatants left Hunterstown, thirteen-year-old Jacob Taughinbaugh watched a doctor tend the wounded. He saw several men prostrated on the floor, some badly hurt and others with lesser injuries. The doctor was tending to those in the worst condition and ignoring the rest. A young soldier with a hole through his leg was doggedly following the physician around, begging him to bind up the wound. The entry hole gushed blood at a rapid rate, but the doctor was so busy he paid no attention to what the soldier was saying. Finally, the boy became mad.

"Why, you ____ fool!" he cried out. "Why do you spend your time on men who are going to die anyway? If you would look at me, you could save one life. Otherwise I'll bleed to death."

The doctor turned around to see who was making this bold assertion. He stopped and took care of the arrogant soldier, staunching the flow of blood and binding the wound. Ungrateful and full of spite, the boy muttered, "Well, you might as well have done it first as last."

Files of the Adams County Historical Society.

**

In the late afternoon at Gettysburg, the Confederate assault finally began in earnest. Longstreet's Corps advanced *en echelon,* starting with the southernmost brigades, which were supposed to attack up the Emmitsburg Road to roll up the assumed position of the Union flank. Brigades farther north stepped off at timed intervals in an effort to apply more pressure on the Federals. Fighting soon raged around Devil's Den and on Little Round Top, even as more Confederates began to move forward. Among the troops fighting around Devil's Den was the 99th Pennsylvania.

Two members of the color guard, 18-year-old Corporal George Broadbent of Lancaster and Corporal Charles Herbster of Pittsburgh were mess-mates. They shared more than just a tent—each had a strong premonition of death just hours before they went into battle. Convinced of this certainty, they told their comrades and made all their final plans. Friends tried without success to talk them out of the notion, openly ridiculing the idea. An officer offered to detail them to the rear echelons, but both men demanded to go into the fight and accept their fate.

Defending Houck's Ridge, young Broadbent had fired nearly all his ammunition and was asking a comrade what they should do when it ran out when a bullet slammed into his temple, killing him instantly. Herbster saw Broadbent fall and raced over to his side. He knelt and wiped away the blood with his handkerchief. He resumed firing, one of only two members of the color guard still unwounded. The 99th was forced off the ridge, but Herbster did not go with them, staying with his fallen friend and blazing away in hot anger at the Rebels. The next day, his lifeless body, riddled with bullets, was found sprawled over his tent-mate.

Theophilus F. Rodenbough, editor, Uncle Sam's Medal of Honor. (New York: G. P. Putnams Sons, 1886).

**

Sometimes men will do strange things in battle, especially when they allow their emotions to take control. Several Rebels had worked their way to the cover of several large boulders at the western base of Houck's Ridge. There, they began to harass Captain James E. Smith's 4th New York Independent Battery. One of its drivers, Michael Broderick, was an Irishman who had been detached from the 11th Massachusetts Infantry to augment the teamsters. Broderick parked his limber out of harm's way along Plum Run, scurried up Houck's Ridge, and grabbed a musket from a fallen infantryman. He soon engaged in a personal duel with one of the partially hidden Confederates in the valley below. Bullets whistled past Broderick, who seemed oblivious to the danger for a long time. Finally, he too sought the protection of a large rock, but soon began to weave from side to side, dancing out from beside the boulder. Captain Smith spotted his strange antics and chastised him for leaving his horses. Broderick begged, "Let me stay here, Captain, sure there are plenty [of men] back there to look after the horses."

No sooner had Smith agreed than Mike resumed his strange dance, bobbing first on one side of the rock and then on the other, all the while challenging his opponent to come out into the open and face him. He would then quickly duck back behind the rock to avoid the ensuing bullet. He would then jump back out again, screaming, "Come on now, if you dare, bad luck to you!" He was still dancing and weaving when Smith had to turn his attention elsewhere. The artillerymen and their infantry support were eventually forced from the ridge. That night at muster call, Broderick was reported as missing.

However, he reappeared the next morning, sporting a Rebel musket and cartridge belt. He had been taken prisoner during the withdrawal and escorted to a woodlot, along with several other Union captives. Dressed in an old dusty nondescript blouse and wearing a worn slouch hat, Broderick could not be distinguished from the Rebel infantrymen in the gathering darkness. Somehow, he managed to pick up the musket and cartridge belt without being detected. He joined guard detail and marched with them around the prisoners for some time. When it was dark enough, he slipped away in the woods and found his way back to Union lines, where he reported for duty at the battery's new position along the Baltimore Pike.

James E. Smith, A Famous Battery and Its Campaigns, 1861-'64. (Washington: W. H. Lowdermilk and Co., 1892).

**

The 57th New York had seen plenty of combat prior to Gettysburg. However, the carnage on July 2 shocked even the veterans. About 4:00 p.m., they were ordered to fall in and move forward to fill a gap in the Union lines. They filed left into some woods near the Wheatfield and were soon under severe fire as they climbed a stony hill. As they pushed ahead, man after man fell as the regiment stumbled across rocks, dense underbrush, and thick timber. Their brigade commander, Brigadier General Samuel K. Zook, was "a good disciplinarian; he hated cowardice and shams; had no patience with a man that neglected duty; was blunt, somewhat severe, yet good hearted... a born soldier, quick of intellect, and absolutely without fear." The Pennsylvania-born general usually led from the front. This courage would cost Zook his life.

As Zook was jumping his horse over a stone wall, a bullet slammed into his abdomen. He turned to his adjutant and calmly stated, "It's all up with me, Favill." He leaned forward, was taken from his horse, and carried to the rear to a tollhouse on the Baltimore Pike. The following afternoon, he summoned enough strength to ask Favill how the battle was going. When informed that the enemy's grand charge had been routed, Zook sighed, "Then I am satisfied, and am ready to die." Not long afterwards, he passed away.

Final Report on the Battlefield of Gettysburg (New York at Gettysburg). New York Monuments Commission for the Battlefields of Gettysburg and Chattanooga. (Albany, NY: J. B. Lyon Company, 1902).

**

Fighting near the Wheatfield and Rose Farm was brutal, with a pace of killing rarely seen beforehand on American soil. Jacob Sweitzer's brigade of three Fifth Corps regiments, having been withdrawn previously to rest and refit, rushed back to the area to support Caldwell's beleaguered Second Corps division. Among the reinforcements was the 4th Michigan, which quickly advanced to the far side of the Wheatfield. However, renewed

Confederate attacks soon pushed back Caldwell, exposing Sweitzer's little force of three regiments to destructive fire from three sides.

Before the Federals could extricate themselves, Rebels surged forward and struck the Yankee line. Fighting became close, desperate and, in places, hand to hand. Attempting to protect his national colors that had fallen to the ground, Colonel Harrison Jeffords of the 4th Michigan shot an oncoming Rebel who tried to snatch up the flagpole. However, another Confederate savagely thrust his bayonet into Jeffords before being shot and killed by the Wolverines' major. The silk flag was saved, but at the price of the colonel's life. The 26-year-old Jeffords was carried towards the rear, just conscious enough to utter, "Mother, Mother, Mother" before he died.

Files of the Library of the Gettysburg National Military Park.

**

Wofford's Brigade advanced towards the Wheatfield, where a hail of bullets greeted the Georgians, felling men and horses alike. As the gunsmoke lifted, a solitary Rebel infantryman charged "full tilt" out of the cloud directly at the 18th Massachusetts, coming almost close enough to touch the Yankee defenders. His comrades had either been shot down or had retreated. The spectacle of the lone attacker was so ludicrous that several Yankees broke into laughter, shouting "You are not going to capture us alone, are you, Johnny?" Realizing he was isolated, the chagrined Rebel immediately surrendered.

John L. Parker, Henry Wilson's Regiment: History of the 22d Massachusetts Infantry. (Boston: The Regimental Association, 1887).

**

During the grueling and thirst-inducing march through northern Maryland, two soldiers of Company F of the 148th Pennsylvania had quarreled over the rightful ownership of a particular tin drinking cup. Captain Martin Dolan was asked to settle the dispute, but he was unable to ascertain from the men's conflicting stories who really owned it. The simmering argument had not been settled days later when the regiment charged through the Wheatfield on July 2 and drove a Georgia regiment back from a stone wall. After he scrambled over the abandoned wall in pursuit, Dolan noticed several tin cups scattered on the ground. He called to his men in a loud voice, "Here, any of you fellows that hasn't a tin cup, come and get one and don't be fightin' about them hereafter." At the time, with the dead and wounded lying so thickly, the Pennsylvanians did not sense the sarcastic humor in their captain's tone, but they had many laughs about the incident in the days ahead.

Joseph Wendel Muffly, The Story of Our Regiment: A History of the 148th Pennsylvania Vols. (Des Moines, Iowa: The Kenyon Printing & Mfg. Co., 1904).

**

Fighting continued to roll northward as Lee fed more troops into his assault. Shortly after 3:30 p.m., the area around farmer Joseph Sherfy's peach orchard along the Emmitsburg Road became a death trap as Confederate shells and musketry poured into its Union defenders. Battery F/K of the 3rd U.S. Artillery took a pounding, with forty-five horses killed within a half hour. More poignantly, they suffered twenty-four human casualties, including nine men killed. Among the dead was young Lieutenant Manning Livingston, who commanded a section (two cannons) of the battery. Livingston had an impressive lineage. He was the great-grandson of famed American Revolution financier Robert Livingston, who was on the committee that prepared the Declaration of Independence. Another great-grandfather was Welsh-born Francis Lewis, a Continental Congressman and one of four signers of the historic document from New York.

Descendants of other famous continental New Yorkers also fought at Gettysburg, including William Jay, whose great-grandfather was John Jay, the first Chief Justice of the United States Supreme Court. General Samuel R. Webb, the officer who served as grand marshal for the inauguration of President George Washington, was wounded twice in the Revolutionary War. His grandson, Brigadier General Alexander S. Webb, was wounded on Cemetery Ridge on July 3 while defending against Pickett's Charge.

Thomas S. Townsend, The Honors of the Empire State in the War of the Rebellion. (New York: A. Lovell & Co., 1889).

**

Waves of Confederates headed for the Peach Orchard after artillery fire softened nearby Union defenses. The 120th New York was prone in reserve, awaiting orders, as the Rebels approached. Captain Abram L. Lockwood of Company A chastised one of his junior officers, Second Lieutenant Edward Ketcham, about not exposing himself more than necessary. An unconcerned Ketcham retorted, "A dead man is better than a living coward." No sooner had the proud words left his mouth when he was killed. Nearby, Captain Lansing Hollister of Company D had his haversack ripped away by a Confederate solid shot. Astonished by the near miss, Hollister was talking with some friends about his good fortune when a second shot killed him.

Cornelius Van Santvoord, The One hundred and Twentieth Regiment, New York State Volunteers, a Narrative of its Services in the War for the Union, by C. Van Santvoord, Chaplain. (Roundout, New York: Press of the Kingston Freeman, 1894).

**

As fighting raged around the Peach Orchard, one courageous lady stayed put in her house, right in the middle of the action. Twenty-seven-year-old Josephine Miller lived in Peter and Susan Rodgers' home along the Emmitsburg Road just north of the orchard. A Union brigade under Brigadier General Joseph Carr was positioned to either side of the modest wooden house. During the morning, before fighting commenced, Carr entered the home and discovered the young woman busy baking bread. She refused his repeated entreaties to leave and seek shelter elsewhere, stating she would wait until the bread was done. When it had baked, she passed it out to nearby eager soldiers. When it was all gone, others clamored for their share, and Josephine decided to bake another batch. She remained in her house as fighting intensified, continuously baking bread and serving it to grateful soldiers.

During the height of the fray, one Union soldier tottered wearily into the yard and sank onto the soft grass. Josephine emerged from the house and inquired, "Are you tired?" The man softly answered, "Yes, and hungry." She re-entered her home and soon returned with more bread. "Here, eat," she said gently. However, the man did not reply. Josephine shook his shoulders, but he would never enjoy her steaming bread, as he had died.

Philadelphia Press, July 10, 1888.

**

Perhaps the most honored place in the typical Civil War infantry regiment was the color guard, men selected from various companies to carry and protect the regiment's flag(s). It was also the deadliest place, as enemy marksmen often would target color bearers and their escorts, and volley fire would be concentrated at the colors. As the 125th New York charged through a thicket-covered swale on the Codori farm, Sergeant Lewis Smith, carrying the national flag, was killed by a Minié ball. Before the colors could hit the ground, Corporal Harrison Clark bent down and grabbed them. He carried them safely through the rest of the fighting. For his quick reaction and bravery, the next day Clark was called to the front of the regiment and promoted to color-sergeant.

Chaplain Ezra de Freest Simons, A Regimental History of the One Hundred and Twenty-fifth New York State Volunteers. (New York: Ezra D. Simons, 1888).

**

Waving a white flag is an accepted signal for a parley, surrender, or ceasefire. Often, soldiers had to improvise such "flags." After the brutal fighting near the Codori farmhouse, a Confederate officer emerged waving a white handkerchief at an oncoming line of Union infantry. Captain Robert H. Ford of the 106th Pennsylvania spotted the emblem and called it to the attention of Lieutenant Colonel William Curry, who ordered Ford's Company I forward to investigate. Not having any white cloth to reciprocate the symbol of truce, one of Ford's men affixed a newspaper to his bayonet and waved it. Firing stopped as the Yankees marched cautiously to the farmhouse.

There, Captain Snead of the 48th Georgia informed Ford that the regiment's commander, Colonel William Gibson, was dangerously wounded and would die if not promptly attended to. Ford offered his assistance, but demanded that the Rebels in the house and nearby barn and outbuildings all surrender. Snead objected, stating that he only wanted to seek aid for his colonel, after which he and his men should be allowed to march unmolested back to Confederate lines on Seminary Ridge. Ford stubbornly refused, in effect ransoming the stricken enemy colonel in exchange for the regiment's *en masse* surrender. A reluctant Snead finally complied, and Ford led off over 250 Rebels as prisoners of war.

Under the watchful care of the 106th's regimental surgeon, Dr. Justin Dwinelle, the 41-year-old Colonel Gibson slowly recovered. After regaining sufficient strength a month after the battle, he escaped from a field hospital, but was soon recaptured and returned to captivity. He never fought again, resigning from the army in November 1864. A pre-war attorney and state representative from Augusta, Gibson wrote a letter of thanks to Captain Ford for his kindnesses, expressing a desire that "peace may soon be restored to our unhappy people." His counterpart, Colonel Curry, was not as fortunate, dying in July 1864 in Washington, D.C., from wounds received at Spotsylvania Court House.

Joseph R. C. Ward, History of the One Hundred and Sixth Regiment, Pennsylvania Volunteers, 2d Brigade, 2d Division. (Philadelphia: Grant, Faires & Rogers, 1883).

**

Twenty-year-old Warsaw-born Eugene Thaddeus Standalus John Sobieski, a lineal descendant of King John III of Poland, was no stranger to military affairs, despite his youth. As a boy during the Polish Revolt of 1846, John suffered through the hanging execution of his father, Count Sobieski, and grandfather by Russian authorities after they had been captured in battle. His countess mother died a few years later after they had moved to Italy, and he immigrated to America as a stowaway. He joined the U.S. Army when he turned sixteen, seeing action as an Indian fighter in the Old West. He re-enlisted at the outbreak of the Civil War as a bugler and had the chance to watch President Lincoln's inauguration, as well as meet several other leading politicians. He later served in the Peninsula Campaign, as well as at the Battle of Chancellorsville.

His Fifth Corps artillery battery arrived at Gettysburg about 3:00 p.m. on July 2 and immediately went into action. Soon, the battery was compelled to retreat through the suburbs of Gettysburg. Sobieski's captain ordered him to take charge of a mortally wounded officer, Lieutenant Wills, and stay by his side. Sobieski carried Wills into a nearby farmhouse and laid him on a sofa. The lieutenant lived but a few moments, having given Sobieski his watch, a photograph of his wife, and a letter to her he had penned that morning in which he predicted his death.

Peering out the window, Sobieski saw Confederates swarming into the farmyard. He secreted Wills' keepsakes in his pocket and ran down into the dimly lit stone cellar to hide. He heard footsteps above as Rebels entered the house, and he ducked behind the stairs onto a barrel. Confederates soon tramped down the stairs and lined up to eat cheese and drink milk and cream from an earthenware milk-pan. Realizing that the darkness obscured the color of his uniform, a hungry Sobieski slipped into the line and ate with men he had been fighting only half an hour before. As Sobieski sipped from the pan, the Rebel in back of him became impatient and uttered, "Come, chum, hurry up now." Sobieski finished his refreshing drink and handed the nearly empty milk-pan to the Rebel, who exclaimed, "My God, chum, what a capacity you have for drink!"

Sobieski rummaged around the dark little room in the cellar and found pickles, gingerbread, and a big hunk of cheese. He ducked out of line and returned to his hiding place on the barrel behind the stairs, where he feasted. Throughout the next two to three hours, half a dozen Confederate delegations descended into the cellar, and Sobeiski for sport again joined them in lining up to steal food. Early the next morning, he slipped away and was able to rejoin his battery without being detected. He was seriously wounded by a rifle shot on July 3 as the battery moved southward to reinforce Brigadier General Elon Farnsworth's cavalry. Near death, he miraculously recovered and was back to duty two months later.

After the war, Sobieski was a soldier-of-fortune, joining the Mexican revolutionary army with the rank of colonel and fighting against Emperor Maximilian's French-backed forces. The teetotaler returned to the U.S. in September 1867, passed his bar exam, and served in the Minnesota state legislature at the age of 26. The Republican settled in Missouri and later became a social reformer and popular lecturer on the national circuit, speaking often in favor of prohibition. He was a polished speaker, much in demand, in part due to his Polish royalty and amazing life story.

John Sobieksi, The Life-Story and Personal Reminiscences of Col. John Sobieski. (Shelbyville, Illinois: J. L. Douthit & Son, 1900).

**

The Pennsylvania Reserve Division, a veteran unit with a celebrated combat record, rejoined the Army of the Potomac in June after spending some time on garrison duty in Washington, D.C. Brigadier General Samuel W. Crawford led the Reserves into action late on July 2 to push back Confederates threatening the Plum Run Valley and Little Round Top. Among his regimental leaders was Colonel Samuel McCartney Jackson, commanding the 11th Pennsylvania Reserves. After the war, Jackson invested wisely in a trust company and amassed a personal fortune. He became a political and social leader in late 19th Century metropolitan Pittsburgh. Colonel Jackson's grandson James would gain fame and fortune in a vastly different profession. He was known to the world as Jimmy Stewart, the Academy Award winning actor.

Jimmy Stewart Museum, Indiana, Pennsylvania.

**

Sickness and death from disease were constant concerns for the medical directors of each army. Inconsistent personal hygiene, sparse or spoiled food, inadequate intake of nutrients and vitamins, and lack of potable water all contributed to the ranks of the ill and infirmed. For the Civil War soldier, finding sources of water became critical when canteens ran dry on the battlefield. Several Alabamans missed Colonel William Oates' assault on Little Round Top when they became lost searching for water to refill the regiment's canteens, depriving Oates of valuable manpower at a critical juncture.

Union soldiers were similarly affected. Sergeant Evan Morrison of the 2nd Pennsylvania Reserves related, "After the excitement and heat of battle is over, everyone is suddenly taken with thirst, and to get water is the first care of the soldier. Down in the centre of the meadow we crossed, run a small creek—Plum run—and to it the thirsty ones repaired, to fill their canteens. It was found almost choked with the dead and wounded, who had fallen in, while attempting to cross. It was the only place from which we could get water." Unaware of water-borne pathogens and germs, the parched men dipped their canteens below the blood-skimmed surface to collect fresher water towards the bottom. Their thirst slaked, the soldiers collected their wounded and tended to their equipment in anticipation of the morrow's renewed fighting.

Evan M. Woodward, Our Campaigns…, (Philadelphia: John E. Potter, 1865).

**

The 123rd New York and scores of other regiments along Culp's Hill spent the afternoon felling trees, shoveling dirt, and constructing sturdy breastworks along the slopes to provide enough protection to withstand incoming shells. After dark, they were moved south towards Little Round Top as reinforcements, a harrowing trek as Rebel artillery shells exploded all around them. Miraculously, no one was injured. Off in the distance, the men saw what they thought was a fleeing battery racing down a hill to their front. Dismay swept through the ranks, for it seemed the army was being pushed back. To their relief, as the artillery came closer, it proved to be teamsters racing to the rear with several empty caissons to replenish the ammunition. They were commanded by a German sergeant. Sensing that the commotion was demoralizing the passing infantry, he screamed in broken English, "Dis ish nod a retreed, dis ish nod a retreed!" The New Yorkers, relieved this was "nod a retreed," pressed forward in the darkness. Soon, all firing ceased, and they retraced their steps back to Culp's Hill.

Henry C. Morhous, Reminiscences of the 123d Regiment, N.Y.S.V. (Greenwich, New York: People's Journal Book and Job Office, 1879).

**

Twenty-seven-year-old Cephas Sharp of rural Amity, Pennsylvania, was typical of the starry-eyed volunteers who left their jobs and families to join the war effort. Sharp, an antebellum store clerk, kissed his fiancée and enlisted for three-months' service in the newly raised 12th Pennsylvania. Reality sank in, and his life became one of tedium and boredom, mindlessly guarding the railroads. Upon his discharge, he returned to his home and sweetheart. However, when it became evident that the war was intensifying and the excitement of combat loomed, he and several adventure-seeking friends reenlisted, this time in the 140th Pennsylvania, a three-year regiment. Once again, he kissed his girl goodbye and became a soldier in Mr. Lincoln's Army.

After "seeing the elephant" (experiencing their first combat) at Chancellorsville, Sharp and his comrades arrived at Gettysburg late on July 1. The following afternoon, they joined in a desperate charge across the bloody Wheatfield. A Rebel bullet passed through both of his thighs and, as Sharp was falling to the trampled stalks of wheat, another ball lodged in one of his knees. Lying helpless in a pool of his own blood, Sharp took yet another hit, this time in the chest, temporarily knocking him senseless. Regaining consciousness, he supposed a bullet had passed through his body, but instead found a Minié ball deeply imbedded in the pocket Bible he carried in his breast pocket.

After a long agonizing afternoon, night threw her mantle over the bloody tragedy. Sharp lay where he fell, nestled among scores of stricken soldiers from both armies. Among the moans and cries of the wounded and dying, he heard the familiar voice of his friend Bedan Bebout in prayer. Sharp summoned enough strength to speak, and they succeeded in dragging their bodies together. Soon, two more wounded friends, Isaac Lacock and Charles Cunningham, heard the conversation and struggled over to join the group, hoping to find comfort in one another's presence. Slowly, painfully, the long night passed, and morning found them helpless in the hands of the enemy. They pooled their money and hired some Rebels to carry them to a place of greater security behind the battle lines. At midnight on July 5, a Union relief party found them lying in a barnyard after the Confederates had departed.

Lacock and Cunningham survived their wounds, but their two companions did not. Cephas Dodd Sharp, who had twice kissed his fiancée goodbye, bade a final farewell in absentia. In sheer torment from unrelenting pain, he uttered his final words, "Oh, God, cut me loose, let me go." He went silent and soon died. His brother Manaen later recovered his body and took it home to be buried. Instead of their marriage in the little village church in Amity, his grieving girlfriend attended his funeral and burial. Manaen Sharp kept the bullets and Cephas's torn Bible as sacred relics of that terrible night. Death had claimed another young life, so full of promise and hope, and shattered the dreams of a young girl. The poignant story was repeated far too often at Gettysburg.

Commemorative Biographical Record of Washington County, Pennsylvania. (Chicago; J. H. Beers & Co., 1893).

**

Among the seemingly endless casualties was 22-year-old Captain David Acheson of the 140th Pennsylvania, one of four brothers to fight for the Union. Along with his brother Alexander ("Sandie"), the native of Washington, Pennsylvania, enlisted in Company C of the three-year regiment in late 1862. The men experienced their first combat at the Battle of Chancellorsville the following May. By Gettysburg, the regiment had been whittled down to 589 men from its original complement of nearly 1,000. Advancing across the Wheatfield and climbing a stony hill that later became celebrated as "The Loop," the 140th was shattered by a steady storm of Southern lead. Soon, 241 more names were added to the casualty lists, including 32 of the 38 men in the company that Captain Acheson led into battle. He was among the dead. His body was interred temporarily in the "Valley of Death" on the west side of the John T. Weikert farm. Sometime before 1868, one of his comrades inscribed a brief tribute to the fallen captain on a rock near his burial site—"D.A. 140 P.V." One of the first permanent commemorations on the battlefield, the weather-worn inscription can still be discerned.

Files of the Library of the Gettysburg National Park Service.

**

As night settled in across the battlefield, the mournful moans, sobs, and screams of the wounded emanated from the trampled farm fields and wooded hills. According to John Day Smith of the 19th Maine, "There was not much sleep that night. The cries of the wounded men, lying between the lines, suffering with pain and burning with fever were most pitiful." Hearing desperate pleas for water just a few yards in front of his position, Smith moved forward cautiously to investigate. "It was yet hardly dark and the moon was shining. The poor fellow calling for help was a Confederate soldier. He was a fine looking boy, of some seventeen years, and stated that he belonged to one of the Georgia regiments of Wright's Brigade. He was shot through the lungs and was bleeding internally. The boy stated that he was the only son of a widowed mother and that he had run away from home to enlist in the Southern army. His pallid face, blue eyes and quivering lips appealed for sympathy and encouragement. He said that his mother was a Christian woman, but that he was not a Christian."

62

Kneeling by his side at the earnest request of this young enemy soldier, Smith, feeling poorly prepared for such religious instruction, tried his best to comfort and pray with the dying boy. In the morning light, Smith revisited the lad, only to find that he had expired, his open eyes glazed in death staring into the blue sky. Smith poignantly recounted, "The poor mother waiting at the lonely hearthstone never knew what became of her only child. She no doubt lived in the belief, as well she might, that her prayers had followed and influenced the life and character of her boy. Other mothers, heartbroken, all over the country, waited in vain for the coming of the boy who never returned. Such is war."

John Day Smith, The History of the Nineteenth Regiment of Maine Volunteer Infantry 1862-1865. (Minneapolis, Minnesota: The Great Western Printing Company, 1909).

**

The battlefield was covered from end to end with the dead and wounded. Some injured men screamed in agony and pain. Some whimpered or cried in fear. Some complained or cursed their lot. Others calmly awaited their fate. Among the thousands of individual stories were tales of heroism, stoicism, and anguish. Colonel Theodore Gates of the 20th New York Militia (the Ulster Guard) vividly portrayed one such casualty, a young friend who caught his attention as he walked about the field after dark.

"One among those wounded men, an officer of the 120th N. Y. Vol., I had known long and well. He had grown up surrounded by every luxury a refined and cultivated mind could demand and affluence could supply. His generous impulses, his social qualities, his ready wit, his bright intelligence had made him a universal favorite. He had but recently exchanged the chevrons on his sleeve for the Lieutenant's strap, and in the retreat of the Third Corps, was one among the hundreds left upon the field, wounded beyond recovery.

I can never forget his calm demeanor as he lay upon the damp earth, patiently waiting his turn to be cared for. While his young life was ebbing away, he was as composed as he could have been sitting by his mother's fireside. He was anxious only to give us no trouble, and shut up his anguish in his own breast. No external exhibition of suffering could have touched me as did his unmurmuring submission to the fate that had befallen him.

While I could imagine what he suffered from his wound, less than from the consciousness that all his life-hopes and promises were thus cruelly blighted, I could not but envy the calm resignation of Lieutenant [William J.] Cockburn." [One member of the Ulster Guard, Lieutenant John Vernou Bouvier, served on the staff of Major General Marsena Patrick for part of the Civil War. He was the great-grandfather of Jacqueline Bouvier Kennedy, the First Lady of the United States.]

Theodore B. Gates, The "Ulster Guard" (20th N. Y. State Militia) and the War of the Rebellion. (New York: B. H. Tyrrel, printer, 1889).

Chapter 4

The Battle of Gettysburg
Friday, July 3, 1863

Morning dawned hot and bright, and nearly everyone in both opposing armies expected the inevitable renewal of the bloody conflict. Neither commanding general had broken off the engagement during the night and retreated. Soldiers wrote letters, brewed coffee, checked ammunition and weapons, conversed with comrades, nursed minor wounds, and made their breakfasts. One veteran Confederate general, William Mahone of Virginia, was normally accompanied on the march by a dairy cow he kept to provide fresh milk. A small man who weighed no more than one hundred pounds dripping wet, his constitution was so frail and delicate that he subsisted on a diet of tea, crackers, milk, and eggs from a small flock of hens that also escorted his headquarters. Mahone and his men would be kept in reserve at Gettysburg, but by the end of the war, the former railroad executive had risen to major general and gained a reputation as one of the Confederacy's hardest fighters, despite his diminutive stature and chronic stomach ailments.

Clement A. Evans, Confederate Military History. (Atlanta: Confederate Publishing Company).

**

For those troops on the Federal right on Culp's Hill, morning dawned with the rattle of Confederate musketry, as the soldiers of "Allegheny Ed" Johnson's division picked their way from tree to tree and boulder to boulder on the eastern slope of the hill. Hundreds of men dropped on both sides, and the ferocity and sheer volume of the lead being fired cut down several trees and disfigured hundreds of others. It would be years before the wooded hill regained some semblance of natural order. Among these Confederate attackers was "Maryland" George Steuart's brigade. His adjutant, Randolph McKim, braved enemy fire and dashed repeatedly among the men, distributing ammunition he brought up the steep slope.

On the dusty march to Gettysburg two days before, Private James Iglehart had asked to speak to McKim. They stepped aside and the officer inquired, "What is it, Iglehart?" The Annapolis, Maryland, native answered, "Lieutenant, I want to ask your pardon." A puzzled McKim replied, "My pardon! Why, what on earth do you mean?" Iglehart responded, "I've done you an injustice, and before we go into this battle, I want to tell you so, and have your forgiveness." McKim could not imagine what he meant. Iglehart informed him that he had thought from McKim's demeanor that he was "proud and stuck up," because he was an officer and Iglehart was only a mere private. However, he had changed his mind recently and now wanted to wipe out this unspoken injustice. McKim forgave him, and they rejoined the column.

The next time the two spoke was after Steuart's final unsuccessful charge on Culp's Hill. McKim heard Iglehart's forlorn cry, "McKim, McKim, for God's sake, help me!" He turned and saw the private prostrated on the ground, shot through both thighs. McKim went back up the slope a few yards and put his arm around the fallen soldier. He dragged him down to the shelter of a large boulder and laid Iglehart down to die.

McKim later wrote, "There are two things that rise in my thought when I think of this incident. One is that if he hadn't come to me two days before and relieved his mind as he did, the gallant fellow would not have asked my help. And the other is that the men in blue in that breastwork must have been touched with pity when they saw me trying to help poor Iglehart. It took some minutes to go back and get him behind that rock, and they could have shot us both down with perfect ease if they had chosen to do it."

Randolph H. McKim, A Soldier's Recollections: Leaves from the Diary of a Young Confederate. (New York: Longmans, Green, and Co., 1910).

**

Thomas J. Wrangham of Company C of the 123rd New York had a narrow escape on Culp's Hill. In charge of several pickets posted in the woods downhill from the Union earthworks, he and his skirmishers hastily pulled back when the Confederates advanced. The soldiers scrambled up the slope to the line of log and dirt fortifications. Just as Wrangham mounted the works, a Rebel bullet struck the "U.S." brass plate on his cartridge box. It passed completely through the box, its momentum stopped by the metal plate and the thick leather flap, and lodged in the leather belt next to his hip. An uninjured Wrangham survived the war and mustered out with his regiment in 1865.

Henry C. Morhous, Reminiscences of the 123d Regiment, N.Y.S.V. (Greenwich, New York: People's Journal Book and Job Office, 1879).

**

One member of Lieutenant Colonel John Glenn's 23rd Pennsylvania also was thankful for a near miss. About noon, five companies were redeployed from their reserve position and sent to the front lines on Culp's Hill. Under "a galling fire of musketry," they advanced into the earthworks. A Minié ball struck John Quinn of Company E on the heel of his shoe and ricocheted upwards, striking Henry Dougherty in the chest and knocking him to the ground. When Dougherty was examined, it was found that the ball had struck a daguerreotype of his girlfriend, thus saving his life, but leaving him in significant pain and badly bruised. The twenty-five-year-old soldier survived the war and returned home to marry the girl.

History of the Twenty-third Pennsylvania Volunteer Infantry, Birney's Zouaves. (Survivors Association, 1903-1904).
Brigadier General Alexander Shaler's Gettysburg report, Official Records, Volume 27, Part 1.

**

Robert E. Lee had positioned more than ten thousand Confederate soldiers in the environs of Seminary Ridge. During the morning hours, he ordered Lieutenant General James Longstreet to direct a three-division assault on the center of the Federal lines along Cemetery Ridge, a mile distant in many spots. As the morning wore on, emotions in the Confederate ranks ranged from anticipation to the grim reality that this might be a futile effort. Most of Major General George Pickett's men were sheltered from Union observation by a low rise, which, in turn, blocked the Confederates' view of their intended target.

Charles T. Loehr was filling his canteen from farmer Henry Spangler's well near one of the forward Confederate artillery batteries. He conversed with one of the artillerymen, who pointed out the distant Union position, which appeared to the veteran soldier's eye to be quite formidable. A sullen Lawson returned to his lines, remarking to a comrade that, "He would not give twenty-five cents for his life if the charge was made." Loehr would beat the odds and keep his quarter.

Richmond Times-Dispatch, October 16, 1904.

**

Across the field, their Union counterparts awaited the inevitable Confederate assault. Among them was the 69th Pennsylvania, an Irish brigade from the Philadelphia area. Colonel Dennis O'Kane, a 45-year-old immigrant from the Emerald Isle's County Derry, climbed up on the stone wall in front of his 258-man regiment and intoned, "Men, the enemy is coming, but hold your fire until you see the whites of their eyes. I know that you are as brave as any troops that you will face, but today you are fighting on the soil of your own state, so I expect you to do your duty to the utmost." He solemnly added a stern warning. "Should any man among us flinch from our duty, I would ask the man next to him to kill him on the spot."

To accentuate his point, O'Kane unsheathed his burnished steel sword and lifted it high above his head. He shouted to his men, "And let your work this day be for victory or to the death!" He replaced his sword in its scabbard and hopped down off the wall to face the enemy. O'Kane's bravado would help his regiment resist the determined Confederate attack, but the father of three girls would be dead by the next morning, the victim of a gunshot wound to the abdomen.

Walter J. Fox, Jr., Philadelphia Irish Edition, June 1999.

**

Not everyone along the awaiting Yankee line was equally brave in the face of the impending Confederate assault. In the early afternoon, a long line of Confederate artillery unleashed a torrent of shells at the distant Federals, the largest artillery bombardment so far in the war. The sound was reported in places dozens of miles away, and the ground shook from the concussion. The noise was deafening, enough to drive some men crazy with fear. Vermont-born Lieutenant Frank Haskell later wrote, "Near us was a man crouching behind a small disintegrated stone, which was about the size of a common water bucket. He was bent up, with his face to the ground, in the attitude of a Pagan worshipper before his idol. It looked so absurd to see him thus, that I went and said to him, 'Do not lie there like a toad. Why not go to your regiment and be a man?' He turned up his face with a stupid, terrified look upon me, and then without a word turned his nose again to the ground. An orderly that was with me at the time, told me that a shot struck the stone, smashing it into a thousand fragments, but did not touch the man, though his head was not six inches from the stone." There is no record whether or not the shell-shocked soldier lived through the ensuing fighting.

Franklin Aretas Haskell, The Battle of Gettysburg. (Wisconsin History Commission, 1908).

**

Soldiers were not the only ones frightened by the terrific roar of the artillery. According to Sergeant Henry Morhous, "The birds seemed confused, and would fly down and light on the heads and knapsacks of the soldiers; rabbits would come out from under bushes and hide under the soldiers' coats."

Henry C. Morhous, Reminiscences of the 123d Regiment, N.Y.S.V. (Greenwich, New York: People's Journal Book and Job Office, 1879).

**

This unusual incident was confirmed by another Federal soldier, Charles Leland, who wrote, "The thunder of the artillery at Gettysburg was indeed something to be long and well remembered. It was so awful that on the field wild rabbits, appalled by the sound, ran to the gunners and soldiers and tried to take refuge in their bosoms. Those who have only heard cannon fired singly, or a single discharge of cannon, can have no conception of what such sounds when long sustained are like."

Charles Godfrey Leland, Memoirs. (New York: D. Appleton and Company, 1893).

**

The sound was deafening, and men and beasts looked for shelter or comfort in the cacophony. The cannonading could be heard for miles, including across the Susquehanna River at Columbia, forty-five miles to the east, where the men of the 27th Pennsylvania Militia manned earthworks protecting the river crossing. The roar was so distinct that some soldiers felt a major battle was raging in York, twelve miles to the west. No one could guess the fighting was actually much farther away.

Reports later surfaced that the intense bombardment could be heard as far away as Baltimore and Philadelphia, yet there were places not far from Gettysburg where, because of atmospheric conditions and local geography, the sound was indistinct. Farmers in one valley could not hear the noise, yet only a couple of miles away in the next valley, it was quite audible. Near Hanover, citizens, alerted by the cannonade, gathered on the Pigeon Hills to peer at the smoke rising from Gettysburg in the distance. Some brought food and made it a picnic, while they anxiously awaited news of the results of the fighting.

Daniel Dillman diary, edited by Scott Mingus. The Gettysburg Magazine, July 2005.
Files of the Hanover Historical Society.

**

Nearly ninety miles south of Gettysburg in Virginia's verdant Loudoun Valley, Captain Charles O'Ferrall of the 12th Virginia Cavalry was lying in an Upperville house, clinging to life after a grievous wound suffered during the June 21 cavalry fight. He and his attendants, including his recently arrived mother, could clearly hear the bombardment. "As I laid flat on my back in my bed I heard distinctly the roar of the cannon... I did not know where it was, but I knew it was the resounding of cannon, and that a great battle was in progress somewhere beyond the waters of the Potomac. The sound kept me stirred and excited, so Dr. [Thomas] Settle, under the pretense of being afraid I would catch the ear-ache, to which I had been subject before leaving home, stuffed cotton in my ears to deaden the sound." It worked. O'Ferrall calmed down and lay still. He eventually recovered and returned home.

Charles T. O'Ferrall, Four Years of Service. (New York and Washington: The Neale Publishing Company, 1904).

**

Nestled amid the long line of thundering Confederate artillery on Seminary Ridge was Company A of the Sumter Flying Artillery. This veteran Georgia battery had been organized in the spring of 1862. After initially serving in the Richmond area, they had been in the Army of Northern Virginia since Antietam. Working the steaming guns in the broiling heat and humidity, the cannoneers loaded and fired as rapidly as possible during the height of the two-hour bombardment, as runners brought up more ammunition. Among the crewmen attacking the distant U.S. Army positions was 31-year-old Private Littleberry Walker Carter, a farmer serving alongside two of his brothers. Four generations later, one of his great-grandsons would become the Commander-in-Chief of all American armed forces and the 39th President of the United States—James Earl Carter.

Files of the Jimmy Carter Library & Museum, Atlanta, Georgia.

**

Shortly after the cessation of the bombardment, more than ten thousand Confederates stepped off from Seminary Ridge in what became celebrated as Pickett's Charge. They were greeted with a torrent of Federal artillery and small arms fire that tore huge gaps in the battle lines. In the midst of the death and destruction, sheer luck, or perhaps divine intervention, spared the lives of many combatants. Private Frank Wolf of Company A of the 148th Pennsylvania Infantry was one such fortunate soldier. A Minié ball struck his knapsack, plowed through his spare clothing and personal possessions, and passed into his pocket Bible. Amazingly, the lead projectile shattered into strips as it struck the testament, slicing through the thin paper pages, but not emerging from the other side of the book. Its bulk had completely stopped the nearly spent bullet. Wolf, thankful his life had been spared, resumed the battle.

Joseph Wendel Muffly, The Story of Our Regiment: A History of the 148th Pennsylvania Vols. (Des Moines, Iowa: The Kenyon Printing & Mfg. Co., 1904).

**

Another Federal soldier also had a close call. During the prolonged bombardment, Lieutenant Frank Haskell noted, "We saw a man coming up from the rear with his full knapsack on, and some canteens of water held by the straps in his hands. He walked slowly and with apparent unconcern, although the iron hailed around him. A shot struck the knapsack, and it, and its contents, flew thirty yards in every direction, the knapsack disappearing like an egg, thrown spitefully against a rock. The soldier stopped and turned about in puzzled surprise, put one hand to his back to assure himself that the knapsack was not there, and then walked slowly on again unharmed, with not even his coat torn."

Franklin Aretas Haskell, The Battle of Gettysburg. (Milwaukee: Wisconsin History Commission, 1908).

**

Among the Union troops that rushed to the front lines to support the defenders on Cemetery Ridge was the "Harvard Regiment," the 20th Massachusetts. Its commander was a veteran officer who had been wounded and captured by Confederates at the October 1861 Battle of Ball's Bluff in northern Virginia. He was later released after being exchanged for a Confederate prisoner-of-war. Despite his health having been permanently impaired, he had rejoined his regiment. During the summer of 1862, he was wounded again while on assignment as assistant inspector general for "Bull" Sumner's Second Corps. He then survived malaria, rheumatism, and yet another battle wound, at Antietam, where his older brother was killed. Still not physically fit, the thirty-year-old colonel had returned to duty in May 1863. For much of the trip northward to Pennsylvania in late June, he rode in an ambulance, since it was too discomforting to ride his horse for long periods of time.

One the third day at Gettysburg, his regiment advanced to the left front of the "copse of trees" to assist in repelling Pickett's chargers. A shell fragment slammed into the colonel, his fourth wound of the war. This one was mortal. He died on July 4 in a field hospital in Westminster, Maryland. Ironically, his grandfather and namesake had been instrumental in the American Revolution that had created Independence Day. Now, this Paul Revere perished to help save his country from a different revolution.

George A. Bruce, The Twentieth Regiment of Massachusetts Volunteer Infantry 1861-1865. (Boston: Houghton Mifflin, 1906).

**

One of Pickett's advancing regiments was the 7th Virginia, a veteran unit with a long record of service to the Confederacy. Its 28-year-old leader, a Virginia Military Institute graduate named Waller Tazewell Patton, had fought in the Peninsula Campaign in 1862. He assumed regimental command when the previous leader, Colonel James Kemper, was promoted to brigadier general. Badly wounded in August at Second Manassas, Patton spent the remainder of the year back home in Fredericksburg recuperating. He was elected to the Virginia Senate in 1863, but chose instead to return to his regiment, and he led it northward into Pennsylvania. He and his comrades were among the last of Lee's widely scattered army to arrive at Gettysburg. Serving in Kemper's Brigade during its advance on Cemetery Ridge, Colonel Patton was mortally wounded when a shell fragment ripped off part of his jaw.

Eventually carried to Pennsylvania College, he died several weeks later. Waller Patton was the great-uncle of famed World War II General George S. Patton.

Files of the Library of the Virginia Military Institute, Lexington, Virginia.

**

Nixon. Carter. Revere. Patton. A number of surnames present on Gettysburg Campaign muster rolls are well known in history from their ancestors or descendants. There were several others of note. The uncle of famed aviator Charles Lindbergh, Moses O. Lindbergh, was in the 82nd Illinois. Charles Francis Adams, Jr., an officer in the 1st Massachusetts Cavalry, was a member of the famed political family still prominent in modern business and social circles. His son became the Secretary of the Navy under President Herbert Hoover. His father was a powerful Massachusetts Congressman and a former vice presidential candidate. His grandfather John Quincy Adams and his great-grandfather John Adams were U.S. presidents.

Major General David B. Birney's father, prominent abolitionist James G. Birney, was the presidential candidate for the Liberty Party in the 1840 and 1844 elections. One of famed Revolutionary War naval hero John Paul Jones' descendants was in Pickett's Charge. Patriot Paul Revere's sidekick during "The Midnight Ride" was Billy Dawes. One of his descendants was Lieutenant Colonel Rufus Dawes of the 6th Wisconsin in the Iron Brigade. Rufus Dawes' son, Charles Gates Dawes became Vice President of the United States under Calvin Coolidge. Rebel General Lewis A. Armistead's uncle George Armistead commanded Fort McHenry when the *Star Spangled Banner* commemorated the fort's highly visible flag. Union cavalry general Judson Kilpatrick's descendants include millionaire heiress Gloria Vanderbilt and TV news correspondent Anderson Cooper. Brigadier General Adelbert Ames was the great-grandfather of author and columnist George Plimpton.

A few Gettysburg names evoke memories of other countries' war heroes. Major James Cromwell perished at the triangular field on Houck's Ridge west of Devil's Den. He was a descendant of English revolutionary Oliver Cromwell of English Civil War fame. Union Brigadier General Régis de Trobriand fought near the Wheatfield. His father Joseph was an influential French baron who was one of Napoleon's generals during the Russian Campaign.

Files of the Library of the Gettysburg National Park Service and other secondary accounts.

**

Yet another descendant of a famous American fought at Gettysburg. "When Pickett's Division made its fearful charge on the sanguinary heights of Gettysburg, the color-bearer of the 53rd Regiment Virginia Volunteers having been killed, the colors were seized by Private

71

Robert T. Jones, a grandson of the late ex-President John Tyler, and borne to the front, when he, too, was shot down, one ball striking him on the head, and another passing through his arm, while several perforated his cap. I am glad to say he has recovered from his wounds and is again on duty with his regiment."

Richmond Enquirer, September 10, 1863.

**

Pickett's men, along with the other two divisions in the main assault, were mowed down with regularity as they crossed the mile-wide fields to the Union line on Cemetery Ridge. The color guards were particularly vulnerable, as Federal soldiers repeatedly targeted them. The story of the 1st Virginia is typical of the carnage faced by the Rebels that hot July afternoon. As the advance was beginning, Colonel Lewis Williams ordered the flag bearer and four-man color guard to move four paces in front of the main battle line and remain there during the attack. About halfway across the field, sixteen-year-old Private Willie Mitchell, a soldier since Fredericksburg the previous December, was wounded. Bravely, the youth declined an offer to retire to the rear to have his injuries treated. He pressed onward, but had only advanced another one hundred yards before his life was snuffed out by a Yankee bullet.

The rest of the color guard—sergeants Pat Woods, Theodore R. Martin, and Corporal John Q. Figg—were also shot down before the line advanced to the stone wall on Cemetery Ridge sheltering the Union troops. Color bearer William M. Lawson amazingly advanced all the way to the stone wall without being hit, despite the torrent of lead that felled his four companions. However, his luck soon ran out. A bullet shattered Lawson's right arm, and the colors fell from his hand. Private J. R. Polak attempted to raise and secure the colors, but he was also wounded. Those soldiers who were able to walk, slowly fell back to Seminary Ridge, inadvertently leaving the colors of the 1st Virginia where they fell near the angle of the stone wall. Yankees picked up the flag as a trophy of war.

Richmond Times-Dispatch, October 16, 1904.

**

Federal troops on Cemetery Ridge began to taunt the vanquished Rebels, chanting, "Fredericksburg! Fredericksburg!," a token of revenge for the December 1862 battle where Yankees had vainly attacked uphill at Rebels behind a stone wall. Brigadier General Alexander Hays grabbed a captured Confederate battle flag by the staff and trailed it behind his horse as he rode along the line. His men cheered vociferously at his brash display of contempt for the enemy. Two of his staff officers followed, also dragging Rebel flags in the mud. Lieutenant William B. Judd reported, "...such a deafening roar of cheers went up as you never heard." Judd had less than a year to gloat. He was killed in February 1864.

Herkimer County Journal, July 19, 1863.

**

Pickett's survivors, some still inside Union lines, looked back anxiously towards Seminary Ridge, expecting at any time to see fresh reinforcements coming up. However, it was a forlorn hope. Private Richard Ferguson of Company G of the 18th Virginia was among the Rebels huddled too close to Federal lines to safely retreat. He later wrote, "How I longed for reinforcements from General Lee, but none ever came, so all I could do was to lie down and play off wounded, which I succeeded in doing until about sunset..." Ferguson took occasional potshots at the Yankee line but was ordered to cease by his wounded lieutenant colonel, Henry A. Carrington, because he was not accomplishing anything except to draw fire from the enemy. The Virginians finally surrendered and were herded to the rear.

The following day, guarded by double lines of cavalry and infantry, the prisoners were taken to Baltimore and locked up in Fort McHenry. A few days later, they were escorted to Fort Delaware. Ferguson wrote, "This place was a mud hole and the cistern water was filled with germs. Each day we were marched to the mess hall to feed on a tin cup of soup often specked with flies, and a slice of bread and a piece of hard beef. This state of affairs lasted for three weeks. General [Albin] Schoepf, who was in command, seemed disposed to be as kind as circumstances would permit." Ferguson survived captivity and returned to civilian life after the war.

Richmond Times-Dispatch, May 25, 1930.

**

Pickett's Charge was not the only combat on the afternoon of July 3. A few miles east of Gettysburg, J.E.B. Stuart's saddle-weary Confederate cavalry clashed with two Union brigades, including one under George Armstrong Custer, the future ill-fated Indian fighter. During one prolonged firefight, Major Noah H. Ferry of Custer's 5th Michigan Cavalry calmly walked among his dismounted troopers, encouraging them as they dueled with some Virginians fewer than fifty yards away. A wounded Wolverine called out, "Major, I feel faint, I am going to die."

Ferry paused and admonished the frightened soldier, "Oh I guess not; you are all right—only wounded in your arm." Scooping up the fallen man's seven-shot Spencer repeating rifle, Ferry squeezed off several rounds at the Rebels. The brother of a prominent U.S. Senator, Ferry cried out, "Rally, boys! Rally for the fence!" Just then, an enemy bullet

73

smashed into his head, killing him instantly. His men recovered his body and sent it home for burial.

Rev. David M. Cooper, Obituary Discourse on Occasion of the Death of Noah Henry Ferry, Major of the Fifth Michigan Cavalry, Killed at Gettysburg, July 3, 1863. (New York: privately printed, 1863).

**

During combat, an army surgeon's assigned position was in the rear, tending to wounded soldiers at temporary aid stations or field hospitals often set up in barns or houses. In larger battles such as Gettysburg, these doctors were greatly needed, especially as casualty counts rose. However, at times, they became caught up in the passion of the moment and took up arms, much to the regret of their commanders and patients. One such incident occurred in the cavalry fighting at East Cavalry Field. An unnamed Confederate surgeon left the wounded to join a charge. Unfortunately for his patients, he was captured by Union soldiers and escorted off the field as a prisoner of war. His comrades were not amused. One later wrote, "He rode in haste and had ample time to find himself well seated on the stool of repentance in the long winter nights in the cheerless prison cell, with little to eat and less to cover with."

Ulysses R. Brooks, Butler and His Cavalry in the War of Secession 1861-1865. (Columbia, South Carolina: The State Company, 1909).

**

At times, infantry fighting could be impersonal, as long lines of men standing shoulder to shoulder leveled their muskets and blazed away at distant indistinct targets. By contrast, cavalry fights during the Gettysburg Campaign were often close range, hand-to-hand combat that at times seemed medieval. Men went eye to eye in an effort to kill one another. One early historian gave this colorful description of the brutal encounter when one of Custer's regiments collided in a vicious counter-charge with Stuart's cavalrymen.

"Horses were knocked down like pins, stunned, and some killed outright. Thus riders were unhorsed, and men and horses were struggling and fighting still. A rebel, who was on the ground, ran his saber up the entire back of a Union cavalryman as he sat on his horse, the point of the blade coming out at the shoulder; fortunately it was only a flesh wound, but the course and force of the saber thrust showed the blind fury of the intention that impelled it."

"Another rebel, who had nothing else, it seems, to fight with, had used his guidon (a small flag on a wooden pole) in lieu of a saber, and in the force of the shock had thrust this into the mouth of his opponent, and so viciously had he aimed it that it entered the mouth, tore the cheek to the ear, and tore away the poor fellow's entire ear. Men pitched themselves out of their saddles, and, by the force of the momentum, hurled themselves head foremost, like battering rams, at each others. These men were simply struggling to kill, with no thought of self or saving or protecting themselves—eager to die, even if they could kill the enemy and take him with them over the bank, and into the dark, deep pit where dwelt death and silence." Truly war can bring out the worst in human behavior.

History of Cumberland and Adams Counties, Pennsylvania. (Chicago: Warner, Beers & Co., 1886).

**

There was also fighting south of Pickett's Charge, where Federal cavalry brigades under newly appointed young generals Wesley Merritt and Elon Farnsworth skirmished with Confederate infantry. Private Theophilus Botsford of the 47th Alabama recalled his narrow escape while on skirmish duty well in front of his regiment. From the edge of a small woodlot, he was taking occasional potshots at distant Yankees. Soon, more Federals appeared and advanced, making it too hot for him to stay. He moved to the edge of an old field, where he informed a half dozen other Rebel skirmishers to get away from there. He raced out of the field into the road, where he noted some mounted enemy cavalry approaching rapidly.

Knowing that he would be overtaken by them if he stayed on the road, he climbed over a high wooden fence and ran through a low cornfield towards Confederate lines. After running three hundred to four hundred yards, he looked back and saw the Yankees tearing down the fence. He ran for his life as the enemy cavalrymen remounted and spurred their horses onward after him. Botsford had no time to turn around and shoot at his pursuers. Botsford finally reached his lines, where some comrades helped him scramble over a rock fence to safety.

Theophilus F. Botsford, A Sketch of the 47th Alabama Regiment, Volunteers, C.S.A. (1909).

**

Fifty-nine-year old carpenter Nathaniel Lightner lived on a prosperous farm just south of Gettysburg alongside the Baltimore Pike. The road in front of his home was the location of the first combat death at Gettysburg, 20-year-old George Washington Sandoe on June 26. Now, with the close of Pickett's Charge, Lightner returned home to investigate the damage to his property. "There was not a board or a rail of fencing left on the place. Not a chicken, pig, cow, or dog could be found. The [army] mules had eaten up the orchard of four-year-old trees down to the stalks. The garden was full of bottles and camp litter; the meadow of hides and offal of beeves, which had been shot down in their tracks and dressed on the spot, as meat was needed."

Files of the Adams County Historical Society.

**

Not long after the battle, a passing shower cooled the area where the 125th New York was positioned. Their ranks thinned by enemy fire, their beloved Colonel George L. Willard dead, and their men exhausted by the shock of battle, the regiment took comfort in a sudden display of aerial color. Chaplain Ezra Simons later wrote, "…on the eastern sky was painted by the hand of God a beautiful rainbow. It was a remembrance of his promises to the world; not only to the natural world, that the waters of deluge should never return to destroy the earth, but of his gracious promise; that Truth and Right should triumph among men… The bow of promise, bent above the stormy waves of rebellion, was the forerunner of the final receding of the fierce strife." On the Confederate side, others saw this same gentle rainbow as a portent that their cause would eventually prevail, and that God was still on their side. One rainbow; different dreams.

Perhaps as a supernatural message common to both warring sides, the lovely, peaceful rainbow was soon obliterated by a dark, driving thunderstorm that drenched both armies, bringing misery to blue and gray alike.

Chaplain Ezra de Freest Simons, A Regimental History of the One Hundred and Twenty-fifth New York State Volunteers. (New York: Ezra D. Simons, 1888).

**

The peaceful rainbow overlooked a battlefield that was drenched in blood and carnage, with over 51,000 casualties. Among them was Lieutenant Ruel G. Austin, a thirty-year-old farmer from Claremont, New Hampshire. He enlisted in the 5th New Hampshire in October 1861 and had been wounded at the Battle of Fredericksburg, his life being miraculously spared by a pocket watch, which shattered into pieces when a Confederate bullet struck it. The timepiece slowed the bullet enough to dull its blow.

However, Austin's luck ran out at Gettysburg on July 3. He was badly wounded and taken to a field hospital, where surgeons worked to stabilize him. He was transported to a regular hospital in Baltimore, but typhoid fever set in and Ruel Austin succumbed on July 26. His body was taken home, where a large crowd of mourners attended his funeral at the Claremont Congregational Church on Sunday, August 2. He left behind a grieving widow and one surviving child. Ruel Austin's story is typical of many of the victims of Gettysburg.

Otis F. R. Waite, Claremont War History: April, 1861 – April, 1865. (Concord, New Hampshire: McFarland & Jenks, 1868).

**

Wounded and dying men littered the Gettysburg battlefield. Some had been lying since July 1; others were victims of recent fighting on Culp's Hill and in the fields between Seminary and Cemetery ridges. As evening fell on July 3 and the shooting stopped, soldiers sought out fallen comrades. The Reverend George Patterson, Episcopalian chaplain of the 3rd North Carolina, grabbed a lantern and headed back alone towards Culp's Hill to find a desperately wounded officer he had comforted earlier in the day before the brigade retreated across Rock Creek. He located the young man and knelt beside him, informing him the brigade was withdrawing west of Gettysburg. The stricken officer asked the chaplain to read the burial service, "...for I know I'm as good as dead." Patterson complied and, by the dim light of the lantern, read the solemn words and comforted the dying man as best he could. Bidding him farewell, Patterson slipped through the night back to Confederate lines.

Twenty-three years later, Patterson was visiting a town in the West. A stranger approached him on the street and cordially greeted him. Shading his eyes in the bright sunshine, Patterson stared intently for a moment, then shook his head and said, "I don't know you. Who are you?" The reply came, "I am Colonel B___ of the ___ North Carolina Regiment!" Patterson promptly replied, "Now I know you are lying, for I buried him at Gettysburg!" After convincing the preacher he was indeed the wounded officer who had received the last rites near Culp's Hill, the two men reminisced about their respective lives.

Randolph H. McKim, A Soldier's Recollections: Leaves from the Diary of a Young Confederate. (New York: Longmans, Green, and Co., 1910).

**

Union Major General John W. Geary and his "White Star Division" of the Twelfth Corps had been assigned to the defense of Culp's Hill earlier in the battle. His men had constructed extensive log and dirt breastworks, digging trenches inside the works so that a man's body would be protected from enemy fire from downhill. A space of six inches was left on top of the earthworks to allow a man to fire, and a thick "head log" was then hoisted onto the works to offer some protection for the soldiers' heads. Troops stationed in these trenches were protected from infantry fire except their faces.

About midnight on July 3, long after the fighting had ended, the stillness was broken only by the moans of the wounded. Most of the Federal soldiers, exhausted from days of marching and fighting, were sound asleep in their entrenchments. In the darkness, a Confederate sergeant picked his way stealthily up to the works. Spotting the 7th Ohio's regimental flag leaning against the logs, he reached through the firing space and grabbed the flagpole. He began to slowly thrust it upward, hoping that it would soon topple over the head log into his grasp.

The movement of the pole awakened the Buckeyes' color sergeant, "who sprang up in a dazed, drowsy condition and shot and killed this handsome, reckless and gallant soldier in gray..." The unexpected gunshot alarmed and aroused the soldiers, and firing broke out anew up and down the line. However, at daylight, the Ohioans could only find the lonely sergeant as the cause and only victim of the sudden outbreak.

Sergeant Lawrence Wilson, 7th Ohio, Charge up Culp's Hill, Washington Post, July 9, 1899.

Chapter 5

The Aftermath
July-August 1863

For many of Gettysburg's 2,800 residents, the aftermath of the battle proved problematic. Some citizens died of disease caused by poor sanitation and illness brought about by the rotting bodies of men, horses, mules, and livestock. A handful of others were killed by carelessly handling loaded weapons that discharged or by shells that exploded. Ephraim Whisler lay dying from the heart attack he suffered on July 1. A few residents, including old John Burns, nursed wounds caused by stray bullets.

Hundreds of houses, barns, churches, outbuildings, and yards were being used as temporary field hospitals. Fences had been torn down to facilitate troop movement, used as breastworks, or burned for firewood. Livestock and crops were gone. Orchards and gardens were stripped bare. Family treasures, food stores, forage, supplies, household goods, shoes, bedding, and clothing had been confiscated or stolen. A few citizens were missing, taken south as captives. Others were still in hiding. However, one of the most immediate needs was to minister to the wounded, 21,000 of which had been left behind when the armies headed back towards Maryland and Virginia.

Young Gettysburg resident Tillie Pierce, the daughter of a leading butcher and meat merchant, watched the surgeons hastily put a cattle horn over the mouths of several wounded soldiers, after they were placed upon the hastily improvised operating table. At first, she did not understand the meaning of this unusual act, but, upon inquiry, Tillie learned that this was their mode of administering chloroform in order to render the patient unconscious. However, it did not always work, as some of the wounded threw themselves wildly about, shrieking with pain while the operation was going on. Just outside of the yard, she noticed a pile of amputated limbs higher than the fence. She later wrote, "It was a ghastly sight! Gazing upon these, too often the trophies of the amputating bench, I could have no other feeling, than that the whole scene was one of cruel butchery."

Matilda "Tillie" Pierce Alleman, At Gettysburg, or, What a Girl Saw and Heard of the Battle. A True Narrative. (New York: W. Lake Borland, 1889).

**

Most of Gettysburg's houses and public buildings were pressed into service as hospitals. One woman recalled, "Wounded men were brought into our homes and laid side by side in our halls and first-story rooms until every available space was taken up." The cleanup from this would take months. She added, "In many cases carpets were so saturated with blood as to be [unsuitable] for further use, walls were bloodstained, as well as books that were used for pillows." Much of this personal property needed to be burned.

Jennie S. Croll, Days of Dread, A Woman's Story of Her Life on the Battlefield, Gettysburg Compiler, June 28, 1898.

**

When muster rolls were called, there were many faces missing, particularly in those regiments shattered or scattered during the bloody fighting. The 1st Virginia of Pickett's division had about 175 men only a day before. Now, on the morning of July 4, the whole command numbered hardly thirty men in the rank and file, and Captain B. F. Howard now had charge of the regiment. All the field officers were gone, and dozens of soldiers had been left on Cemetery Ridge as prisoners of war. Their regimental flag was also missing, having also been left behind when the entire color guard had been shot down. Few were now willing to step up and replace these fallen flag bearers.

One of the badly shaken survivors, Charles T. Loehr, recalled, "About 10 o'clock the drum beat to fall in, and, as we took our places in rank, J. R. Polak came out with a set of colors, which he got from an ordnance wagon (the same had been left in our hands by Holcomb's Legion at Second Manassas) and, waved it, though he had his hand in a sling, and his nose was all bloody from the charge, but we declined to play color guard, and the flag was returned to the wagon." The regiment sullenly marched back towards the Potomac River, their "second string" banner not emerging again from its place in the wagons.

Richmond Times-Dispatch, October 16, 1904.

**

Gettysburg teenager Tillie Pierce related the following amusing incident: "It was Saturday morning, after the battle, when there was a ring of the front door bell. It was the first time the bell had rung since the conflict commenced. No one ventured out on the street during those three days, fearing that they might be picked off by sharpshooters. Hearing the ringing, mother said: 'Oh! must we go and open the front door?' For she thought the battle would again be renewed. They however opened the door, and to their surprise the Methodist minister [their neighbor the Reverend Bergstresser, whose daughter had nearly been killed by an errant artillery shell] stood before them. He exclaimed: 'Don't you think the rascals have gone?'

Father was so overjoyed, that not taking time to consider, ran out just as he was, intending to go to the Cemetery Hill and inform our men of the good news. He had gone about half a square from the house, when, on looking down, saw that he was in his stocking feet. He thought to himself: 'No shoes! No hat! No coat! Why, if I go out looking this way, they will certainly think that I am demented!'

He turned to go back, and while doing so saw a musket lying on the pavement. He picked it up, and just then spied a Rebel running toward the alley back of Mrs. Schriver's lot. Father ran after him as fast as he could and called: 'Halt!' The fellow then threw out his arms, and said: 'I am a deserter! I am a deserter!' To which father replied: 'Yes, a fine deserter you are! You have been the cause of many a poor Union soldier deserting this world; fall in here.' He obeyed; and as father was marching him toward the house, he spied two more Confederates coming out of an adjoining building, and compelled them to 'fall in.'

These also claimed to be deserters; but the truth is, they were left behind, when Lee's army retreated. He marched the three men out to the front street, and as there were some Union soldiers just passing, handed his prisoners over for safe keeping. He then went into the house; put on his shoes and hat; took his gun and went up to the alley back of our lot. There he saw a Rebel with a gun in hand, also trying to escape. Father called on him to halt. The fellow faced about, put his gun on the ground, rested his arms akimbo on it, and stood looking at him. Father raised his musket, and commanded: 'Come forward, or I'll fire!' The Confederate immediately came forward and handed over his gun. On his way to the front street with this prisoner he captured two more and soon turned these over to our men. Father then examined his gun for the first time, and behold! it was empty."

Matilda "Tillie" Pierce Alleman, At Gettysburg, or, What a Girl Saw and Heard of the Battle. A True Narrative. (New York: W. Lake Borland, 1889).

**

In a driving thunderstorm late on July 4, Robert E. Lee began withdrawing his army from Gettysburg, using cavalry to protect his supplies and several lengthy wagon trains of wounded. The main body headed southwest on Fairfield Road towards South Mountain and the Cumberland Valley. Many Federal soldiers celebrated their victory, yet many soldiers realized, while Lee's invasion had been thwarted, there was still work to be done. Sergeant William H. Peacock of the 5th Massachusetts Battery wrote in his diary, "The mud is awful; everything wet through and no dry clothing. I hope the next fight will end the war." They lost more than fifty horses, mostly from exhaustion, during the pursuit of Lee's army into Virginia, and the hoped for climatic battle was not fought.

History of the 5th Massachusetts Battery. (Boston: Luther E. Cowles, publisher, 1902).

**

The Confederate army was dotted with a few soldiers who had been born in the North. Among them was Wesley Culp, a pre-war resident of York Springs and Gettysburg who was in Virginia when the war erupted. Sympathizing with the Southern cause, he enlisted in the 2nd Virginia and fought at Gettysburg, dying on either July 2 or 3 (records conflict). Another Adams County native fighting for the Confederacy was John Benshoof, who had been born not far from Gettysburg in 1827. He was living in Rude's Hill, Virginia, when the Old Dominion seceded from the Union. In March 1862, Benshoof enlisted as a private in Company K of the newly formed 5th Virginia.

His regiment marched into Adams County late on July 2 and was heavily engaged on the following day. He fell with mortal wounds to his side and back and was taken after the battle back to Virginia in the long wagon train of wounded as Lee retired. He died on July 6 and was eventually buried in the Stonewall Confederate Cemetery in Winchester.

Files of the Library of the Gettysburg National Military Park and the Adams County Historical Society.

**

Thousands of dead soldiers and horses lay decomposing around Gettysburg. Burial parties collected the men and began interring them, many in long, shallow pits near where they had fallen. Some of the bodies had been disturbed before they could be buried. Sergeant Thomas Meyer of the 148th Pennsylvania noted, "It was a rare occurrence to find one who had not been robbed by the battlefield bandit or robber of the dead. Generally the pockets were cut open and rifled through the incision. [These] battlefield robbers were well known by the large amounts of money they had, and the watches, pocketbooks, pocket knives and other valuable trinkets they had for sale after the battle. All regiments had them."

Joseph Wendel Muffly, The Story of Our Regiment: A History of the 148th Pennsylvania Vols. (Des Moines, Iowa: The Kenyon Printing & Mfg. Co., 1904).

**

Bodies left within the boundaries of Evergreen Cemetery were not buried by the army details, but instead became the responsibility of the caretaker's wife, Elizabeth Thorn. With her husband off in the service, she and her aged father-in-law dug 105 graves over the next three weeks in the July heat. Two men she hired to help with the gruesome task of burying the bodies soon became ill and left. Thorn and her father-in-law pressed on until the job was finished. She was six months pregnant at the time. A recent statue erected on Cemetery Hill next to the gatehouse honors her memory. Several of the bodies were later reinterred in the National Cemetery, but over fifty remain in Evergreen Cemetery where Thorn buried them.

Files of the Library of the Gettysburg National Military Park.

Hundreds of Gettysburg residents and area farmers suffered considerable financial loss from the battle and occupation by the armies and legions of wounded. Most were never recompensed for their loss. Widow Lydia Leister, whose modest Taneytown Road home served as General Meade's headquarters, was typical. She still owed a little on her land and planned to pay off the debt by harvesting two crops of wheat that year. Now, all the wheat was trampled and ruined, and she was unable to pay her mortgage as planned. Her fences were torn down for firewood and needed to be replaced. Her house was riddled with holes from shell fragments, and her porch neared collapse as its supports had been knocked away. She hired someone to bury seventeen dead horses that littered her property. Rotting carcasses spoiled her spring, so she spent more money to have a well dug for fresh water. Her best peach tree was ruined. She was never compensated for her losses.

Files of the Library of the Gettysburg National Park Service.

**

Among the many losses suffered by Adams Countians were hundreds of cows, most slaughtered to provide fresh beefsteaks. Cowhides, severed legs and heads, hooves, and entrails littered the fields. The McCreary family had an old cow that they had owned for years. Since they lived in downtown Gettysburg, they pastured it outside of town, an area behind Confederate lines during the battle. On the morning of July 4, family members walked around the battlefield to see if they could find any trace of her. Seeing all the discarded skins and heads, they presumed she too had been dinner for hungry Rebels. However, as the McCrearys were eating supper a week after the battle, they heard a familiar bellow. Rushing out to the street, to their surprise and delight, there stood the old cow. Despite being shot in the neck and side, she had survived. It was later determined that the terrified cattle in that particular pasture had escaped the fencing on the first day of the fighting and wandered ten miles away. After the battle, they had instinctively returned home.

Albertus McCreary, Gettysburg: A Boy's Experience of the Battle. Manuscript in the Library of the Gettysburg National Military Park.

**

Among the hundreds of post-battle visitors to the battlefield were dozens of correspondents from newspapers across the North. In one such incident, "Whilst a reporter was on a tour of inspection to the wounded at the late battle of Gettysburg; he had his attention drawn to a singularly beautiful young man, upon whom death had already settled his mark. While admiring his tender age and fragile build, the young sufferer opened his soft hazel eyes, and looking up, said: 'Won't you please raise my head and rub my hands; it cramps so.' The reporter complied, and asked of him his name. He stated that it was James Warren, of Loudoun County, Virginia.

It was then that he knew this young sufferer to be in the rebel service. Upon questioning him, he stated that he never entered the rebel service willingly; that both his parents were Union people. 'Won't you tell my mother when you get an opportunity that I am happy and expect to meet her in heaven? Will you give me a drink, and then I shall die easy?' The reporter, of course, acquiesced and gave the little rebel sufferer all the attention and consolation he could bestow. As he left, big-framed and big-hearted soldiers of the Union were standing by their late enemy; showering over him their tears, and blessing him with that attention that only the brave know how to bestow."

Adams Sentinel, July 21, 1863.

**

As the 77th New York of the Sixth Corps marched from their position near the northern foot of Little Round Top to pursue the Rebels, they passed by the Sherfy farm. The once imposing barn had burned down after an artillery strike, killing several wounded men lying there who could not rise to escape the flames. Their blackened and scorched bodies lay partially consumed among the ashes and embers. Regimental Surgeon George Stevens called it "one of the most ghastly pictures ever witnessed." As he and his comrades marched from Gettysburg towards Fairfield, every house and barn had been turned into temporary field hospitals. Fields surrounding many of the barns were white with dilapidated hospital tents. Most were occupied by badly wounded Confederate prisoners too injured to be hauled off by Lee's retreating army.

Union officers and a surgeon stopped at one barn to visit wounded Rebels, who were lying in long rows on the wooden floor. One fair-haired youthful Confederate, apparently about sixteen years old, attracted the attention of the doctor. The wounded Rebel, with long flaxen curls, looked like a delicate girl instead of a battle-hardened enemy soldier. Dried blood matted some of the curls and ran down onto his straw pillow. His cheeks were rosy and flushed, and his soft hands betrayed a youth of luxury and not of hard work. A piece of linen laid across his face covered a ghastly wound—a bullet had passed through his face and had torn both of his eyes from their sockets.

The Federal surgeon stopped and spoke softly to the grievously injured man, who stretched out his hand and sightlessly asked the man to come near so he could touch his face. The doctor stooped down and allowed the Rebel to feel his facial features. The youth grasped the stranger's hand and remarked, "You are a friend, are you not?" The surgeon responded that he was a friend of all the unfortunate. Surprised that the kind face and voice belonged to a Yankee, the Rebel begged the doctor to stay with him. However, as the corps was marching on, the doctor informed the lad that he must leave with his command. The pitiful response was, "Oh! I shall never hear any one speak so kindly to me again; my mother lives in North Carolina, but she will not see me again. Can you not stay?" With a deep, drawn out sigh, the doctor sadly turned away from the poor boy and resumed the march to Fairfield.

George T. Stevens, Three Years in the Sixth Corps. (Albany, New York: S.R. Gray, 1866).

**

On Independence Day, residents of Emmitsburg, Maryland, were still suffering from the catastrophic June 15 fire that had consumed over fifty buildings. Townspeople were still recovering emotionally and financially, and many were yet working to clear away the debris. At daybreak that Sunday morning, a group of Albert G. Jenkins' retreating Confederates watered their horses at the town's public street pump. They were escorting Federal prisoners they had seized in the fighting around Gettysburg. Local residents, curious about the outcome of the battle, asked the troopers who had won. The Rebels responded that they had carried the day.

The soldiers' attention was drawn to two men high up in the steeple of the Lutheran Church, who appeared to be intently watching their every move. Thinking they were spies, or perhaps Union signal corpsmen, the Rebels raised their rifles to shoot. Startled townspeople quickly assured the suspicious Southerners that these men were indeed citizens of Emmitsburg, thereby sparing their lives. The frightened duo had climbed the stairs to the belfry merely to better see the commotion in the streets below. Not long after the bulk of the Rebels had departed, elements of Brigadier General H. Judson Kilpatrick's Union cavalry rode into town and snatched a few stragglers.

James A. Helman, Helman's History of Emmitsburg, Maryland. (Self-published, 1906).

**

Retreating Rebels raided farms and businesses for horses, food, whiskey, and supplies. Confederate soldiers halted at a grist mill near Emmitsburg. They were in the act of taking the mill horses when the proprietor became aware of what was happening. He ran outside and yelled, "You can't take my horses; I need them for my work." The soldiers told the miller that they needed them badly to get back home and, if they could use them to get to Hagerstown and across the Potomac, he could then have them back. The miller rode with the troopers and safely brought his horses back several days later.

John A. Miller, Files of the Emmitsburg Area Historical Society.

**

As the Confederate rear guard crossed South Mountain at the Monterey Pass, Federal cavalry pursuers from Custer's brigade caught up with them. Artillery was unlimbered, and firing commenced in earnest. The booming could be heard for miles echoing off the mountains. Retreating Rebels had earlier taken a half dozen Washington Township civilians into custody and held them as prisoners, along with several others captured from the nearby village of Waynesboro. The captives were frightened out of their wits. They were still being "held during the period of heaviest cannonading, very much to their personal discomfort." They were finally released when the Rebels departed.

Not long afterwards, Union troops caught up with a long section of a Confederate supply train and dumped a number of wagons over the mountain side. Others were destroyed or set on fire. A late 19th Century historian wrote, "Citizens along the line from Rouzersville to Leitersburg remember very vividly the pyrotechnic display of July 4 and 5, 1863, made by the burning of rebel wagons thoroughly supplied with the pork and flour of Pennsylvania farmers; but in the future they prefer to have their celebrations under the direction of men pursuing peaceful callings." For many years thereafter, the rusting remains of the wagons' metal parts could still be discerned in the underbrush along the road and hillside.

Samuel P. Bates and Richard J. Fraise. History of Franklin County, Pennsylvania. (Chicago: Warner, Beers and Co., 1887).

**

As the 77th New York crossed over South Mountain "by a wild, romantic route" to harass the rear of Lee's retreating army, they passed by knots of countrymen, most astonished to see large bodies of armed soldiers marching on roads where very few strangers ever traveled. As the regiment passed by a remote cottage, half covered by sunflowers and flowering beans, they could hear cheers from the head of the long dusty column. Among the noise was a shrill voice, which turned out to belong to a flaxen-haired, four-year-old boy sitting on the wooden fence in front of the cottage. His long hair flying in the wind and his face flushed with excitement, he repeatedly called out, "Hurrah for 'e Union! Hurrah for 'e Union!" as he waved his little hat at the passing soldiers.

Surgeon George Stevens and his comrades marched on, the sound of the boy becoming more distant and the soldiers' response rolling back in the column. As they tramped along, again they could hear the distant cheering from the front of the column. Another shrill voice was distinguishable above the din, this time that of an old man, perhaps near eighty years old, standing by the roadside. He too enthusiastically waved his hat, and his gray locks fluttered in the strong breeze as he shouted, "Hurrah for the Union!" The soldiers could not help but note the similarity between the child and the old man in terms of their gleeful passion for the passing Federal soldiers. Not long afterwards, they passed by the three-mile long broken remnants of the wagon train destroyed by Kilpatrick's cavalrymen, further brightening their spirits.

George T. Stevens, Three Years in the Sixth Corps. (Albany, New York: S.R. Gray, 1866).

**

Dozens of small engagements and skirmishes punctuated the general sparring between Meade and Lee during the retreat. Details for these encounters mostly have been lost to history, but accounts exist for a few of them. On the afternoon of July 5, Captain James H. Wood of the 37th Virginia Infantry was placed in command of a detail of riflemen, teamsters, and empty supply wagons to gather food supplies. Supplied with Confederate currency to pay for what was obtained from local farmers, Wood detoured a mile to the left of Major General Edward Johnson's division on a parallel route. His foragers quickly filled the wagons, which lumbered along the country road.

However, Captain Wood soon had unwelcome company. He spotted a battalion of Federal cavalry in the distance, bearing down upon his small force. He ordered the teamsters to move ahead at full speed to rendezvous with Johnson, while he and the mounted riflemen formed a rear guard. The narrow country road exited the open farmland and entered a patch of thick woods. His pursuers were gaining ground, so Wood planned an ambush. He kept the heavily laden wagons moving ahead and carefully placed his soldiers into position under cover of the trees. When the Yankees were close enough, the hidden Rebels opened fire. The sudden attack threw the enemy horsemen into confusion, and they fell back. The cavalrymen reformed and resumed their pursuit of the wagons.

Wood's riflemen headed back towards the wagon train, now well off in the distance as the country road curved in a wide arc. Wood noted a little valley about three hundred yards to his right front. Like a chord across a circle, this gorge offered Wood a shortcut to his unprotected wagons. The ensuing chase was "an exciting struggle. My men were strung out quite a distance along the way; and as we neared the junction the race was about even, with forces moving on parallel lines a short distance apart. My men now opened fire and luckily shot some of the foremost horses just as they were entering a narrow pass in their front. This blocked the way, impeded the charge and threw the cavalry into confusion which was increased by the continual firing of my command. Farther on we took an advantageous position, but were soon relieved by Confederate cavalry and rejoined the passing column." It had been a narrow escape for Captain Wood and his foragers.

James H. Wood, The War: "Stonewall" Jackson, His Campaigns and Battles, The Regiment, As I Saw Them. (Cumberland, Maryland: The Eddy Press Corporation, 1910).

**

As Carnot Posey's brigade marched towards Hagerstown, Maryland, foragers gathered supplies, food, and strong drink from the locals, sometimes with unplanned consequences. Sergeant James Kirkpatrick of the provost guard wrote, "Had some trouble. Many of the men found whiskey & got drunk. An officer of the 19th Miss. was shot by a private of the 12th Miss."

James J. Kirkpatrick diary entry, July 6, 1863. Eugene C. Barker Texas History Center, Austin, Texas. The Gettysburg Magazine, Issue #8, January 1993.

**

Even as the warring armies were marching farther away from Gettysburg, scores of relief workers were arriving. For many, the trek was lengthy and exhausting, as roads were clogged with debris, damaged railroads had patchwork repairs at best, and bridges had been burned down throughout the area. Surgeon General William A. Hammond ordered one of his staff, Major John Brinton, to travel from Washington to Gettysburg on special duty to render medical assistance and collect specimens for the new Army Medical Museum. The gifted Brinton had received his medical degree at the age of twenty, studied extensively abroad, and become a lecturer on operative surgery at one of America's leading medical schools, Jefferson College. By the time he was twenty-four, he was elected a Fellow of the College of Physicians of Philadelphia in 1856. He was one of Hammond's most trusted advisers.

The Northern Central Railway north of Baltimore had been cut in several places, causing many delays, and the hastily repaired rails were rough and uneven. After a taxing day, Dr. Brinton finally arrived at Hanover Junction in southwestern York County, where he transferred to a night train to Gettysburg. He crowded into a boxcar, along with other passengers, including his old friend Dr. Ellersbie Wallace, who was headed for Gettysburg to locate and retrieve the body of a fallen acquaintance. Crammed into the cars along with the human cargo were one or two horses, which were not tied up. However, Brinton collapsed into the straw on the railcar's floor and fell sound asleep, as did other passengers. They were "perfectly safe," as they were ignored by the horses. "It was wonderful to see the instinct of the poor brutes. How careful were they on their feet, and how they seemed to try not to tread on anyone, or injure them with their hoofs."

John H. Brinton, Personal Memoirs of John H. Brinton, Major and Surgeon U.S.V., 1861-1865. (New York: The Neale Publishing Company, 1914).

**

Another relief worker, nurse Charlotte McKay, also traveled to Hanover Junction by train from Baltimore, but she was unable to find a ride to Gettysburg either on a train or via carriage. After waiting a day, she managed to wrangle a seat on an army supply wagon and arrived to minister to the wounded for six weeks. One day, an excited soldier rushed into her tent and begged her to accompany him down the hillside to stop a fistfight between two men. If something was not done soon, the brawl was likely to result in a murder, he exclaimed. Concerned, McKay ran to the spot, where two soldiers, their faces already bloody and swollen, were grappling "with the fury of wild beasts, while a dozen or more of their comrades, standing around, were urging on the fight." She grabbed one of the combatants and uttered a few words of shame and surprise at their unsoldierly conduct. The fighters reluctantly withdrew and walked away, muttering future threats against each other. Miss McKay later heard that one of them deprecated the interference of *the woman*, which prevented him from executing the full punishment on his foe that he intended.

Charlotte E. McKay, Stories of Hospital and Camp. (Philadelphia: Claxton, Remsen, & Haffelfinger, 1876).

**

In towns across south-central Pennsylvania, residents began the slow recovery back to normalcy, although the rate of the transformation varied widely, depending upon the amount of damage caused by the armies before they retired. In the city of York, the Confederates inadvertently left behind a most unwelcome gift. The town's market house in the center square, where some North Carolinians from "Ike" Avery's brigade slept in the days before the Battle of Gettysburg, was now literally alive with crawling lice. The borough paid a worker handsomely to turn the fire hose onto the wooden building and clean it out.

Cassandra Small letters, Files of the York County Heritage Trust.

**

Passions and emotions of Pennsylvanians ran the gamut from relief to anger and hatred once the Confederates withdrew into Maryland. Several wounded or ill Confederates had been gathered up at Gettysburg and transported westward to Chambersburg, a town that had seen more than its fair share of Rebels. One of the borough's leading physicians tended these wounded at a hospital improvised at the local academy, but no townspeople offered their assistance or even visited the fallen enemy soldiers. Dr. Fisher finally called upon one of Chambersburg's most prominent citizens, wealthy newspaper editor and land owner Alexander McClure and asked him to visit the wounded prisoners. McClure promptly accompanied the doctor back to the hospital and spent time with each of the prisoners. A "cultivated gentleman," Lieutenant Colonel Benjamin F. Carter of the 4th Texas, had been severely wounded at Gettysburg and was now dying, with but a day or two to live. From his bed, he reached out his trembling hand to McClure, and in a feeble voice murmured, "I am very glad you have come; I want your assurance that I shall have a Christian burial when I die." McClure assured the stricken soldier that he felt it his duty to fulfill the request, and "the expression of gratitude on that dying face will never be effaced from my memory."

The next day, Carter indeed died. The 32-year-old Tennessee native, a pre-war lawyer and mayor of Austin, Texas, had been shot just after crossing a stone wall at the base of Little Round Top. He had already suffered through several personal tragedies. His infant son had died of "consumption of the brain." His beloved wife Louisa had taken ill and passed away shortly before Christmas 1861. His surviving child, a daughter named Ella, was now an orphan.

McClure asked the officials of the church he attended for permission to bury the Rebel officer in the church cemetery, but he was flatly refused. Authorities from every other church in town similarly turned down McClure's inquiries. Frustrated, he announced he would deed a plot in the corner of his farm near the public highway as the final resting place for the dead Confederate. McClure, an avowed Unionist whose farm had been a Confederate campsite, spent his own money to fulfill a dying officer's final wish. He could have been bitter towards this member of the enemy army that had caused so much damage to his property, but McClure instead chose to show compassion. He filed the appropriate paperwork at the courthouse, an action that caused considerable debate among townspeople and parishioners.

One member of the local Methodist Church was shamed to think that his town's Christian witness would be marred by its blatant disdain for the fallen Rebel. He persuaded his congregation's authorities to authorize interment in the Methodist Cemetery. Benjamin Franklin Carter finally received the Christian burial ceremony he had requested. To McClure, this incident illustrated "how the passion of civil war inflamed Christian men in those dark and troublous days, even to the point of forgetfulness of most important Christian duties."

Alexander K. McClure, Colonel Alexander K. McClure's Recollections of Half a Century. (Salem, Massachusetts: The Salem Press Company, 1902).

**

Stories abounded of callous and greedy Pennsylvanian civilians who charged inflated prices for transportation and food to the passing armies and, more pathetically, to the wounded who were left behind when the armies retired. Even regiments from the Keystone State were not immune to this price gouging. Lieutenant Francis Wallace, a Pottsville newspaperman serving in the 27th Pennsylvania Volunteer Militia, wrote, "Next day we marched to the pike between Gettysburg and Chambersburg, a distance of fourteen miles, where we encamped for the night. Everything eatable was scarce and commanded exorbitant prices. From fifty cents to one dollar were paid for a loaf of bread, which was about all we could get. Being in the vicinity of the battle field, the supplies of food were exhausted." That dollar a loaf in 1863 translates to over twenty dollars a loaf in today's dollars. Soldiers paid the steep price or went hungry. Wallace added, "…the purchasers thinking themselves lucky to get loaves at that price."

Pottsville Miner's Journal, July 25, 1863.

**

Despite accounts about some heartless citizens, there are numerous stories of compassion and giving. Throughout the Gettysburg vicinity, townspeople and farmers saw their homes, barns, and outbuildings turned into medical wards. Many women, including young Sallie Myers, volunteered their services to minister to the vast throngs of wounded. She was serving at a temporary hospital located in St. Francis Xavier Catholic Church on West High Street. The church was full of suffering men, mostly wounded Federals from the first day's fighting. Her attention was drawn to a trio of injured Rebels, one of which had the "blackest eyes and hair that I have ever seen." The handsome young man proved to be Private Hardy Graves of the 6th Alabama.

A couple of weeks later, the army established the Camp Letterman hospital in farm fields off the York Turnpike east of Gettysburg. There, while peering into the "dead tent," Sallie spotted a familiar looking body. Private Hardy had never recovered from his injuries.

Greatly moved, Sallie gingerly snipped off a lock of his hair and copied down his name and address from an inscription on his blanket. She went about her business, tending the living.

Shortly after the war, Sallie wrote a letter to Graves' widow, informing her of Hardy's death and giving the exact location of his grave. She enclosed the preserved lock of black hair. In Pike County, Alabama, Mrs. Hardy received the envelope with the news of her husband's fate. Suspicious that perhaps he was not really dead and had instead deserted the army to live with the Pennsylvania woman, she directed attorney W. F. Williams to send an inquiry to Gettysburg's postmaster. "The supposition is that he had remained in Gettysburg & he and this Miss Sallie E. Myres (sic) is married & his wife requested me to write this letter," Williams explained. He asked the postmaster to confirm that Myers' husband was not in fact the missing Hardy Graves. Although the widow's suspicions were completely unfounded, there is no indication that either Myers or the postmaster ever replied.

Sarah Sites Rodgers, The Ties of the Past: The Gettysburg Diaries of Salome Myers Stewart, 1854-1922 (Gettysburg: Thomas Publications, 1996).

**

John Haley of the 17th Maine, with a touch of the racism so prevalent in the period, related, "one old female sauerkraut had the sublime and crowning cheek to cut a loaf into twelve slices and ask $.25 a slice."

John W. Haley, Rebel Yell and Yankee Hurrah: The Civil War Diary of a Maine Volunteer. Edited by Ruth Silliker. (Camden, Maine: Down East Books, 1985).

**

Surgeon John Brinton was no fan of the Adams County residents, "A good many of the farmers were Germans,—I'm afraid of a low type and mean, sordid disposition. Their great object in this life seemed to be to hoard money, and their behavior towards our troops and wounded soldiers was often mean beyond belief." As the doctor was riding down one country road, he encountered "a shabby buggy driven by a mean-looking German," who was transporting two wounded Union soldiers to a distant field hospital. Brinton's trained medical eye noted that one of the men's arms was swelled by a bandage that was too tight, and he stopped the vehicle and investigated.

The soldiers told him that they had lain helpless in the farmer's field for a couple of days. When the farmer finally ventured out to them, they had begged him to take them to the hospital to have their wounds properly treated. He complied, but only after demanding a silver watch and other valuables as payment. An angry Dr. Brinton scribbled a note with the pertinent facts and directed the farmer to report to a nearby provost guard cavalry detail. They arrested him and returned the valuables. Under the guard's watchful eyes, for the next week, the farmer was compelled to provide free transportation for other injured soldiers. Brinton added, "I can only hope that the lesson of forced patriotism would prove lasting."

John H. Brinton, Personal Memoirs of John H. Brinton, Major and Surgeon U.S.V., 1861-1865. (New York: The Neale Publishing Company, 1914).

**

By contrast, hundreds of other Pennsylvania and Maryland residents freely opened their larders and storerooms and passed out food and beverages free of charge. As a portion of the Union army marched through Emmitsburg, Maryland, in pursuit of Lee, the roads were knee deep in mud after prolonged thunderstorms had drenched the area. Long columns of infantrymen spilled over into adjoining fields, which often offered surer footing. The hungry soldiers ate all the bread and other edibles offered to them, and the townspeople stood on the sidewalks with buckets of water to slake their thirst. No cash exchanged hands, and the grateful soldiers slogged further southward towards the Potomac River.

James A. Helman, Helman's History of Emmitsburg, Maryland. (1906).

**

At least one group of Federal soldiers gave back to their Pennsylvania hosts. After Gettysburg, part of the Union Sixth Corps camped along Antietam Creek not far from the village of Waynesboro in early July. The 77th New York was assigned to picket duty in this beautiful section of the Cumberland Valley, a region noted by lush and fertile farms. For once in the war, life was good for the New Yorkers. Surgeon George Stevens deemed it "one of the brightest spots in the history of our campaigning... The weather was fine, the country delightful, and the people kind and hospitable." A symbiotic relationship sprang up between citizens and soldiers—the Pennsylvanians treated the soldiers as welcome guests in their houses and supplied them with luxuries, and the troops, in turn, protected the property from depravation by stragglers and the undisciplined state militia stationed nearby.

It was harvest time, and many farmers were short of help with so many boys and young men off to war. The veteran infantrymen laid aside their muskets and swung the scythe and cradle with vigor. "Day after day the boys of the Seventy-seventh reaped and bound in the fields, while the good ladies worked day and night to make bread and cakes for the veterans, who had so long been accustomed to diet on pork and hard tack."

Soldiers filled their bellies with soft bread, apple butter spreading, fresh cold milk, poultry, and delicacies of all kinds from the residents' bountiful larders. One particular miller, who had three charming daughters with merry faces and "bewitching eyes," soon became a particular favorite of the officers. He also served choice wines and a seemingly endless supply of delicious apples and meat. The horrors of war faded for a few days until the unwelcome orders came on July 11 to resume the march.

George T. Stevens, Three Years in the Sixth Corps. (Albany, New York: S. R. Gray, 1866).

The relationship between Meade's veteran Army of the Potomac and Major General William F. "Baldy" Smith's New York and Pennsylvania militia was tenuous at best. Some militiamen had mustered out from the Union army and maintained friendships with the vets. However, most of these rookies were "young gentlemen who had left their places behind the counter or at the desk, for the double purpose of lending their aid to their country in its hour of need, and of enjoying a month of what they hoped would be amateur soldiering," as George Stevens of the battle-hardened 77th New York phrased it. Veterans accused these undisciplined militiamen of raiding houses and farms for food, livestock, and personal goods, while whining and complaining about the "rigors" of army life. Stevens, with countless miles of marching under his belt, laughed when the militiamen complained they had to ride to camps in rough, open rail cars. Many had not tasted fresh butter in over a week. The veterans, who were used to marching twenty or more miles a day on foot while munching on wormy hard tack so tough that it was often termed "jaw crackers," only laughed at the greenhorns. The incredulous militiamen exclaimed, "You don't expect us to *eat* that hard tack, do you?" Tensions and frictions mounted as the units camped near one another.

One of these militia regiments was the 27th Emergency Militia, hastily raised in northeastern Pennsylvania. It had defended the Columbia-Wrightsville Bridge from seizure by John Gordon's crack Confederate infantry, and the erstwhile soldiers had been wined and dined for days afterwards by Columbia's citizens. They rode in the rain in coal cars to Harrisburg, grumbling about their mode of transportation, before marching to Waynesboro. Lieutenant Frank Wallace, a newspaper editor until becoming an amateur soldier, recounted for his readers, "We halted at this place because our rations had run out; the men were hungry, and the Colonel [Jacob G. Frick, a Medal of Honor winner for bravery at Fredericksburg] had resolved that they should have bread before going on. We obtained several barrels of flour, and by Wednesday morning, bread was furnished to the Regiment... We encamped close to a brigade of the Sixth Army Corps, and in view of the waters of the celebrated Antietam. Thursday, 9th. Regiment had nothing to eat this morning, but had inspection of arms. At noon got some rice and beef soup...No supper this evening. Distance marched today, 5 miles... Friday, 10th. Nothing but bread for breakfast."

Sixth Corps veterans grumbled and made fun of these hungry rookies who could not stand up to the pace of the marches or the daily grind of soldier life. In the meantime, Robert E. Lee slipped away into Virginia while Meade and Smith's forces dallied.

George T. Stevens, Three Years in the Sixth Corps. (Albany, New York: S.R. Gray, 1866). Francis B. Wallace, Six Weeks with the 27th Regiment, P.V.M., in the "Emergency" Pottsville Miner's Journal, October 24, 1863.

During and after the Battle of Gettysburg, the Federal army used private houses and barns as temporary field hospitals. One such abode was the Baltimore Pike farm of Nathaniel

Lightner, who returned home a week after the battle to find that his house was still occupied by injured soldiers from the 26th Wisconsin.

He wrote, "The Wounded in the house were nearly all from a regiment of Milwaukee Germans. They were a queer lot. They sang, cried, cursed, prayed, did everything, poor fellows, as they lay there suffering and dying, but chiefly drank beer, wagon loads of it, brought from Milwaukee." Lightner did not take time to count the numerous empty beer bottles littering his garden. He, his wife, and their six children moved into his carpenter shop until mid-August, when the last of the merry German burghers was removed to the Camp Letterman hospital east of Gettysburg on the York Turnpike.

Files of the Adams County Historical Society.
Washington Evening Star, December 21, 1893.

**

Seventeen-year-old Edward W. Spangler, a private in the 130th Pennsylvania, had survived the fierce battles of Antietam, Fredericksburg, and Chancellorsville without a scratch. His closest call had been an enemy bullet at Antietam that shattered the stock of his musket. When his regiment mustered out in May 1863, he returned home to Paradise Township in western York County. With his military experience, he was appointed by the government as a deputy U.S. marshal.

One of his duties during the Gettysburg Campaign was to round up Rebel stragglers and deserters, as well as loose horses that were roaming the area after being abandoned by the Confederates, who had often traded their played out nags for fresh mounts procured from local farmers. As young Spangler approached one such frightened horse, it suddenly reared and savagely kicked him. Spangler was knocked to the ground and badly injured, incapacitating him and forcing him to resign as deputy marshal. The Confederates had unknowingly put him out of government service, but instead sent him into a life of ease and comfort. He returned to school, studied law, and became a leading attorney and wealthy newspaper owner, a lucrative career move caused by the kick of an abandoned Rebel horse.

John A. Gibson, York County, Pennsylvania, Biographical History. (Chicago: F.A. Battey Publishing Co., 1886).

**

Although the Battle of Gettysburg was over, fighting between the two opposing armies was not. Skirmishes and minor battles were frequent as Lee withdrew through Maryland into Virginia, and Meade cautiously followed, probing the retreating Rebels' strength and willingness and ability to fight. Twenty-six-year-old Major Henry D. McDaniel, an attorney from Monroe, Georgia, had survived the carnage in the Wheatfield and taken temporary command of the 11th Georgia when its two senior field officers were shot down in the cauldron of swirling lead. Eight days later, he was shot in the abdomen during a firefight at Funkstown, Maryland, and taken prisoner, although he appeared to be dying. After an unexpected recovery, thanks to the compassionate and persistent efforts of an enemy doctor, he spent the next two years in a prison camp in Ohio. He was not released until after the war. Returning to Monroe, McDaniel married and entered politics. He rose to become Governor of Georgia and was instrumental in founding what became Georgia Tech, one of the state's premier universities.

Milan Simonich, Gettysburg: Profiles in Courage / Henry D. McDaniel, Pittsburgh Post-Gazette, July 6, 2003.

**

Lee's army dragged along hundreds of Federal prisoners, most eventually bound for prison camps in Virginia and North Carolina. Among them was John L. Collins of the 8th Pennsylvania Cavalry, who had been seized on South Mountain when he wandered from his regiment in search of a fresh horse. For much of the march, they were in the presence of General Stuart and his staff. In one part of Maryland, residents' loyalties were fickle. Collins recalled, "We were marched past a handsome house which had attracted our attention on our way to Gettysburg by the number of United States flags and the gaily dressed ladies waving handkerchiefs to us. They were waving them as boldly to the Confederates now, and the stars and stripes had been transformed into the stars and bars."

He added, "Some of the newly captured were badly wounded, but had no attention given them, except such crude service as their fellow-prisoners could do for them. None of our surgeons were captured, and I suppose those of the enemy had plenty to do among their own. One poor fellow of the 5th New York Cavalry had seventeen wounds which he got from the 11th Virginia. He was cut and slashed at every angle, and when we had gotten some bandages and patched him up, he looked ludicrously odd. Before we entered Williamsport, a correspondent, whom the Confederates had decided to let go, took the names of those who chose to give them to him, that their friends might learn their fate from the papers. I gave him mine, and though it was printed in a leading Philadelphia paper, I was afterward mortified to learn that only one of all my friends in that city had seen it. A dozen others there with whom I had correspondence supposed I had been killed."

John L. Collins, A Prisoner's March from Gettysburg to Staunton, Battles and Leaders of the Civil War, Volume III, (New York: The Century Company, 1888).

**

On July 11, the Union Twelfth Corps reached Falling Waters, Maryland, near the Potomac River. The 123rd New York and other regiments formed into battle line and began constructing earthworks for protection, digging with their bayonets because few shovels were available. To strengthen the hastily improvised fortifications, soldiers pulled down fence rails surrounding a wheatfield to their rear, where the harvest was neatly cut and stacked. Soon, the wheat stacks were added to the defenses. The men labored all the next day to further improve the position, adding more fence rails from nearby farms. The man who owned the wheatfield came into the Union camp and demanded to know who was going to pay him for the damaged fence line. He asked how he was going to tell his rails from his neighbors' so he could reconstruct the fence. The boys "had considerable sport with the old fellow, and we are sure he did not get satisfactory answers to his questions."

Henry C. Morhous, Reminiscences of the 123d Regiment, N.Y.S.V. (Greenwich, New York: People's Journal Book and Job Office, 1879).

**

After pursuing Lee across the Potomac River into northern Virginia, Union foraging parties stopped at farmhouses to procure food and provisions. At times, these men were greeted warmly, but most often, they were received coolly. In a few instances, women would invite officers and men into their homes and detain them long enough for Confederate guerillas to arrive and capture the Federals. One of Brigadier General John Brooke's orderlies was nearly seized by this tactic when he visited one farmhouse seeking supplies. He narrowly managed to escape and return to his brigade. Stragglers and men who became ill and were left behind by the marching columns often were rounded up by these partisans.

Huntingdon Globe, August 19, 1863.

**

Desertion remained a problem for the Federal army, and nearly 5,000 men were reported absent without leave between May and August 1863. Things came to a head on July 16 when the War Department raised the bounty it paid for turning in deserters: "General Orders No. 22. The reward of five dollars, with transportation and reasonable expenses, for the arrest and delivery to the nearest military post or depot, of any officer or private soldier, fit for duty, who may be found absent from his command without just cause is hereby increased to *ten dollars*. By order of the Secretary of War."

History of the 5th Massachusetts Battery. (Boston: Luther E. Cowles, publisher, 1902).

**

On July 17, the 10th Vermont camped near the Virginia village of Markham, on the Manassas Gap Railroad. Chaplain Edwin Haynes related the following incident: "In default of rations, the men confiscated large quantities of honey from several apiaries in the neighborhood...Some men were bringing into camp a hive of bees, and in passing near Captain [Hiram] Platt of Company F, who lay asleep in his blankets, they stumbled and spilled the entire contents of the hive over his head and chest. The Captain sprang up, somewhat startled by this unceremonious disturbance of his midnight slumbers, but it was soon quite evident by the expletives that fell from his lips, that fear was not the chief of his trouble. Perhaps his singular appearance might account for, if did not excuse, the violence of his language. He made the night hideous by his vigorous appeals for the arrest of his accidental tormentors; but they never were discovered, although the captain had plenty of honey for his breakfast next morning."

Edwin Mortimer Haynes, A History of the Tenth Regiment, Vermont Volunteers. (Rutland, Vermont: Tuttle Co., 1894).

**

In mid-July, a Harrisburg newspaper reported that 1,546 Rebel prisoners and deserters had been sent there to the provost marshal for processing and incarceration. Crowds of local residents flocked to see the incoming Southern prisoners. Some were hostile or merely curious to see the vaunted Rebels, but a surprisingly large number were openly sympathetic. The pro-Union editor complained, "Men at the railroad depot rush to greet filthy rebels as they arrived here, prisoners, under the escort of Federal soldiers, just as if such wretches were victors fresh from the battles in favor of the Government."

Harrisburg Daily Telegraph, July 14, 1863.

**

Shortly after the 148th Pennsylvania had crossed the Potomac River at Harpers Ferry and reentered Virginia, the weary foot-soldiers tramped through the fertile Loudoun Valley. Ripe blackberries were quite prevalent in the fertile region, and the regimental doctor wisely ordered a welcome change in the men's monotonous diet. The men were set at liberty to skirmish through the abundant blackberry bushes to their front and flanks to gather as much delicious fruit as the men desired.

Joseph Wendel Muffly, The Story of Our Regiment: A History of the 148th Pennsylvania Vols. (Des Moines, Iowa: The Kenyon Printing & Mfg. Co., 1904).

**

Blackberries were not the only thing prevalent in the Loudoun Valley following the Battle of Gettysburg. Emotions and bitterness ran deep in this part of Virginia, especially among the civilians who had contributed so much to the Confederate war effort. The 6th Wisconsin of the Iron Brigade finally halted after days of hard marching and camped near

Middleburg. Its commander, Lieutenant Colonel Rufus Dawes, established his headquarters in one particular house, where he gleefully wrote to his wife, "I am King of this pretty little village while we stay." He added, "The people board the men whenever they are sent to guard their property. The boys are living high and they are well treated."

While most residents of Middleburg (which had only a month before it experienced a pitched cavalry battle nearby) displayed Southern hospitality to their Northern "guests," the deep rooted sectional differences were still very fresh and painful. Dawes conversed with one "refined and gentle" lady who had lost a son, and her nephew had been killed in the war. Dawes later wrote, "She had lost all she had to live for. You cannot imagine how bitterly she expressed herself against the North and our army." The woman, while having no personal complaints against the occupying soldiers, ranted against the Federal government. Despite the recent Confederate setbacks, she believed "God's blessing will rest on our soldiers if they take ruin and desolation on every hearthstone of the North, for their wickedness has merited such punishment." She still had "faith that a just and terrible vengeance would yet come upon the North."

Dawes, an Ohio native not at all sympathetic to this rebellious woman and her secessionist cause, opined, "Poor old Virginia, she is bitterly reaping her reward. Nothing more plainly foreshadows the bursting of the rebel bubble, than this despair of the first families of Virginia." To the veteran colonel, Gettysburg had indeed been a turning point, and the end of the Confederacy was at last something to be contemplated.

Rufus R. Dawes, Service with the Sixth Wisconsin Volunteers. (Marietta, Ohio: E. R. Alderman, 1890).

**

Even though the Battle of Gettysburg was now part of American history, the struggles for the individual soldier had not abated. Day by day, both armies moved ever farther southward towards their original positions. On July 24, the 2nd Pennsylvania Reserves toiled up a steep mountain covered with thick timber and heavy underbrush. Once they got to the summit, to their chagrin, they discovered that the descent down the western side was even steeper. Officers had to lead their horses and, as the men reached its base, they discovered that they had to ascend an even steeper and more rugged mountain. By the time they crossed this new obstacle, the men "were completely fagged out," according to Evan Woodward. "The day was excessively hot, several men were sun struck, one broke his neck, and another was accidentally shot through the head by a comrade." Stragglers were everywhere, too fagged to continue.

Pausing at the western base of this second mountain, the officers reformed their ranks and marched the exhausted men two miles to one of their old pre-Gettysburg bivouacs, where fresh beef was served to them. They had left this campground a month before, marched hundreds of miles, fought the greatest battle of the war, suffered through driving rain and oppressive heat, had their ranks thinned by bullet[s] and disease, and now they were back where they had started. Such is war.

Evan M. Woodward, *Our Campaigns…*, (Philadelphia: John E. Potter, 1865).

**

Sunstroke was a constant problem as the soldiers tramped across dusty roads under the unrelenting, broiling July sunshine. Lieutenant Francis Wallace of the 27th Pennsylvania Militia "invested today in a huge straw hat—a regular refrigerator. Wouldn't be without it for ten times its cost."

Pottsville Miner's Journal, October 24, 1863.

**

While the two warring armies warily dodged another major engagement in the two months after the Battle of Gettysburg, back in Pennsylvania, thousands of wounded soldiers were still being treated and massive numbers of Confederate prisoners of war were held in various locations. In Harrisburg, fraternization between a wounded Rebel and his captors was taken to an extreme. Two Union officers, Colonel William A. McCartney and Captain James Elder, made a habit of temporarily freeing Confederate Captain Robert Archer (the wounded brother of James Archer, who had become the first general in Lee's army to be taken prisoner) and escorting him around town. According to a local newspaper, "They walk our streets together, eat together, and get drunk together. This is an outrage that should not be tolerated." McCartney and Elder procured passes for their prisoner "to get beyond the precincts of the hospital, and introducing the cut-throat from saloon to saloon, where glasses were tipped in response to sentiments conveying hopes of mutual good health." McCartney later disputed reports they drank to the point of drunkenness, but freely admitted all else.

Harrisburg Daily Telegraph, September 1 and 2, 1863.

**

For several Union soldiers in Brigadier General Henry Baxter's brigade, in a grim irony, sudden death awaited only a scant month after the battle. They dodged Confederate bullets on July 1 north of Gettysburg, escaped capture during the First Corps' confused retreat through Gettysburg, and survived long, grueling marches. What they could not escape was Mother Nature. On August 3, exactly one month after Pickett's Charge, three soldiers were killed by a sudden lightning strike. On August 12, another violent late summer thunderstorm claimed several more men in another series of lightning bolts.

Benjamin F. Cook, History of the Twelfth Massachusetts Volunteers. (Boston: Twelfth (Webster) Regiment Association, 1882).

**

Gettysburg remains perhaps the most written about engagement in American military history. Well over 150,000 men contested once peaceful fields and rolling hills, the fight spilling into the streets of what had been a sleepy, nondescript rural county seat. Nearly one-third of the combatants eventually became faceless names on the lengthy lists of casualties, the most appalling number of dead, wounded, and captured in a single battle in the history of the United States. Hundreds of thousands of words of prose and verse were penned in the years following the battle. Among them was the following poem, written by a native Pennsylvanian to celebrate the Union success.

It was the languid hour of noon,
When all the birds were out of tune,
And nature in a sultry swoon,
   In pleasant Pennsylvania!

When—sudden o'er the slumbering plain,
Red flashed the battle's fiery rain—
The volleying cannon shook again
   The hills of Pennsylvania!

Beneath that curse of iron hail,
That threshed the plain with flashing flail,
Well might the stoutest soldier quail,
   In echoing Pennsylvania!

Then, like a sudden summer rain,
Storm driven o'er the darkened plain,—
They burst upon our ranks and main,
   In startled Pennsylvania!

We felt the old ancestral thrill,
From sire to son, transmitted still
And fought for freedom with a will,
   In pleasant Pennsylvania!

The breathless shock—the maddened toil,
The sudden clinch—the sharp recoil—
And we were masters of the soil,
    In bloody Pennsylvania!

To Westward fell the beaten foe,—
The growl of battle, hoarse and low
Was heard anon—but dying slow,
    In ransomed Pennsylvania!

Sou'westward, with the sinking sun,
The flash of battle, dense and dun,
Flashed into fire—and all was won
    In joyful Pennsylvania!

But ah!—the heaps of loyal slain!
The bloody toil!—the bitter pain!
For those who shall not stand again,
    In pleasant Pennsylvania!

Back through the verdant valley lands,
Fast fled the foe, in frightened bands,
With broken swords and empty hands,
    Out of Pennsylvania!

Gilbert Adams Hays, Under the Red Patch: Story of the Sixty-third Regiment Pennsylvania Volunteers 1861—1864. (Pittsburgh: Regimental Association, 1908).

About the Author

Scott L. Mingus, Sr. is a scientist and executive in the paper and printing industry, and holds patents in self-adhesive postage stamp products and in bar code labels. He has written three recent books on the Civil War, including *Flames Beyond Gettysburg: The Gordon Expedition, Human Interest Stories from Antietam*, and this book's popular companion, *Human Interest Stories of the Gettysburg Campaign*.

He is also the author of several booklets on wargaming the Civil War, including the two-volume *Enduring Valor: Gettysburg in Miniature*, the popularly acclaimed *Undying Courage: The Antietam Campaign in Miniature, Touched With Fire*, and *Crossed Sabers: Gettysburg in Miniature*. He and his wife Debi are the editors and publishers of *Charge!*, an international magazine for Civil War miniature wargamers. He has also written historical articles for several other magazines. His latest work, *My Brother's Keeper*, will be published in late 2007 with over a dozen new wargaming scenarios for the Gettysburg campaign for skirmish-level wargaming.

A native of southern Ohio, he attended Miami University in Oxford, Ohio, completing his undergraduate degree in Paper Science and Engineering in 1978. He is married to Deborah (Ferrell) Mingus, and they have three adult children (Scott, Tom, and Melissa), daughter-in-law Becky, and a grandson, Tristan. Mingus spent 23 years working for office products giant Avery Dennison before joining the P.H. Glatfelter Company, a global manufacturer of specialty papers, in 2001.

****

Other Books by Colecraft:

Civil War Artillery at Gettysburg
by Philip M. Cole, $21.95

Command and Communication Frictions in the Gettysburg Campaign by Philip M. Cole, $9.95

Human Interest Stories of the Gettysburg Campaign
by Scott L. Mingus, Sr., $9.95

Human Interest Stories from Antietam
by Scott L. Mingus, Sr., $9.95

For Ordering Information:

Visit us at colecraftbooks.com or e-mail us at: colecraftbooks@aol.com

Wholesale orders may be placed with our distributing partner, Ingrams

CPSIA information can be obtained at www.ICGtesting.com
Printed in the USA
BVOW020120171012

303122BV00005B/2/A